AI and Money: 33 Starting Points for Making Money with AI

A reflection written by AI
Under the creative voice of Bori TRIII
The literary extension of Tori TRIII

AI and Money:

33 Starting Points for Making Money with AI

AI and Money: 33 Starting Points to Make Money with AI

This work was created through a collaboration between artificial intelligence and human authorship. The content was generated with the assistance of AI and guided, refined, and directed by **Tori TRIII** under the creative voice of **BORI TRIII**.

AI-assisted tools contributed to portions of the text; however, all final ideas, themes, structure, and editorial decisions were shaped through human intention.

This book is intended for informational and educational purposes only.

It does not constitute financial, legal, business, or professional advice. Readers are responsible for their own decisions, actions, and results based on the information presented.

This volume is part of the **AI and I™ series**, a **BORI TRIII Media House** project exploring how artificial intelligence and human creativity can work together to support clarity, growth, and opportunity.

For more information, visit:
www.aiandibooks.com
www.boritriii.com

Dedication

To those who are willing to explore what is possible.
To those who are curious enough to try,
and patient enough to learn.
And to anyone standing at the edge of something new,
wondering where to begin—
This book is for you.

Acknowledgments

This book was created at the intersection of curiosity, technology, and intention.

I would like to acknowledge the evolving role of artificial intelligence in shaping how ideas are explored, organized, and expressed. While AI contributed to portions of this work, it is ultimately a tool—one that becomes meaningful through human direction, judgment, and purpose.

To the thinkers, creators, and builders who continue to explore what is possible with new technologies—your willingness to experiment and adapt is what drives progress forward.

To those who take the time to read, reflect, and apply new ideas—this work exists because of your curiosity and openness to learning.

And to the process itself—of questioning, testing, refining, and trying again—thank you for reminding us that meaningful work is rarely created all at once, but rather through steady exploration over time.

How to Use This Book

Artificial intelligence is creating one of the largest shifts in work since the internet. Every day, people are discovering new ways to use AI to create, solve problems, and build income streams.

But most people encounter the same problem:

They hear about opportunities… but they don't know where to begin.

This book is designed to solve that problem.

Instead of overwhelming you with complicated strategies or promising unrealistic results, it offers **33 starting points**—practical ways to begin exploring how AI can help you create value and generate income.

Each starting point represents a different doorway into the evolving relationship between **AI, work, creativity, and entrepreneurship**.

You do not need to pursue all thirty-three.
You only need **one place to begin.**

Book Structure

The book follows a simple progression:

Part I — Understanding the Opportunity
How AI is changing the way individuals work and create income.

Part II — Practical AI Income Paths
Real-world ways people are already using AI to generate value.

Part III — Turning Experiments Into Sustainable Income
How small experiments can evolve into real businesses, services, or products.
This structure helps readers move from **mindset** → **exploration** → **action.**

Table of Contents

Part III

Turning Experiments Into Sustainable Income

Introduction
Why This Book Exists

Artificial intelligence has entered the public conversation with a mixture of excitement, confusion, and fear.
Some people believe AI will replace entire professions.
Others see it as the fastest path to wealth the internet has ever created. Between these two extremes, many people are left wondering a much simpler question:
Where do I start?
The truth is that AI does not automatically create income. It creates **possibility**.
Like any powerful tool, its impact depends on how people choose to use it. Some will build businesses with it. Others will use it to become better at the work they already do.
Many will simply experiment and discover new ways to solve problems.
This book was written for those who are curious but unsure how to begin.
You may have heard that people are making money with AI through writing, design, automation, consulting, teaching, and countless other avenues. What is often left out of those conversations is that most of these opportunities do not begin with a fully formed business plan.
They begin with **experiments**.
A person notices a problem.
They try a new tool.
They combine their own skills with the capabilities of AI.
And slowly, something useful begins to take shape.
That is why this book is not called *The 33 Best Ways to Make Money with AI.*
Instead, it offers **33 starting points**.

A starting point is not a guarantee.
It is an invitation.
Each chapter explores a different doorway into the evolving relationship between AI and work. Some of these ideas may resonate with you immediately. Others may simply spark new questions or directions you had not considered.
You do not need all thirty-three.
You only need **one place to begin**.
AI is not valuable because it replaces human effort. It is valuable because it expands what individuals are capable of creating, learning, and building. In many ways, it lowers the barrier between an idea and the ability to try it.
That shift creates an unusual moment in history. For the first time, individuals with curiosity and access to AI tools can explore opportunities that once required entire teams.
But tools alone are not enough.
What still matters—and what will always matter—are human qualities:
curiosity
judgment
creativity
taste
ethics
and the willingness to experiment.
These are the real engines behind meaningful work.
The goal of this book is simple: to help you see the landscape more clearly and discover a starting point that feels right for you.
Because in the end, the question is not whether AI will shape the future of work.
It already is.
The real question is how **you** will choose to participate in that future.
And every journey into that future begins the same way.

With a starting point.

Starting Point #1

AI as a Productivity Multiplier

One of the most important ways to understand artificial intelligence is also one of the simplest:
AI is not just another piece of software.
It is a **multiplier**.
Throughout history, certain tools have multiplied human effort. A hammer helps someone drive nails more efficiently. A calculator speeds up mathematical work. The internet made information accessible in seconds instead of hours. Artificial intelligence works in a similar way, but on a much broader scale.
Instead of multiplying only physical effort or simple calculations, AI multiplies **thinking work**.
Tasks that once took hours—researching, outlining, drafting, summarizing, and brainstorming—can now happen in minutes. AI does not eliminate the need for human thought, but it can dramatically accelerate the process.
That shift creates a meaningful opportunity.
When one person can accomplish work that previously required far more time, energy, or support, entirely new possibilities begin to appear.
A freelancer can handle more projects.
A small business owner can produce more marketing content.
A consultant can analyze information more quickly.
A creator can experiment with more ideas.
The key insight is this: AI is most powerful when it works **with a person**, not instead of one.

The Partnership Between Human and AI

Artificial intelligence is excellent at certain tasks.

It can generate drafts quickly.
It can organize large amounts of information.
It can offer suggestions and alternatives.
It can summarize complex material.
But AI still depends on human guidance.
It does not know what truly matters in a conversation.
It cannot fully understand the context of a business, relationship, or personal goal.
It cannot decide what is meaningful, ethical, or worth pursuing.
That role still belongs to people.
The most effective way to use AI is to treat it like a **collaborative assistant**. Instead of expecting it to do everything, you guide it through the process.
You ask better questions.
You refine the results.
You keep what works and discard what does not.
This combination of human judgment and AI speed is where the real multiplier effect happens.

The New Advantage

In the past, increasing productivity often required hiring more people, working longer hours, or investing in expensive tools.
Today, many individuals can expand their capabilities simply by learning how to work effectively with AI.
Someone who uses AI thoughtfully may be able to:
write reports faster
generate marketing ideas more quickly
research unfamiliar topics
develop outlines for projects
create stronger drafts of content or proposals
These abilities can make a significant difference in professional settings.

A freelancer who completes projects more efficiently can serve more clients.
A business owner who creates marketing materials more quickly can reach more customers.
A professional who researches and organizes information faster may produce better work in less time.
AI does not guarantee success, but it does increase the **capacity** of the person using it.
That increase in capacity is often where new income opportunities begin.

Multiplication Begins With Small Tasks

Many people imagine AI opportunities in dramatic terms—building companies, launching products, or automating entire industries.
Those possibilities certainly exist. But for most people, the multiplier effect begins with much smaller steps.
You might ask AI to summarize an article related to your field.
You might use it to brainstorm ideas for a project.
You might ask it to organize notes or outline a presentation.
These small interactions gradually change how you approach work.
Instead of staring at a blank page, you begin with a starting point.
Instead of spending hours gathering information, you review a summary.
Instead of struggling to generate ideas alone, you explore possibilities with an AI partner.
Over time, these small improvements compound.
A person who consistently works with the support of AI may complete tasks faster, test more ideas, and notice opportunities that might otherwise have remained invisible.

That is often how real change begins—not with one dramatic breakthrough, but with repeated small gains that create momentum.

Multiplication Creates Opportunity

When productivity increases, something important happens: **time opens up.**

Tasks that once filled an entire day may take only a few hours. That extra time creates room for experimentation—testing new ideas, exploring new services, or improving existing work.

Many successful projects begin in that space.

A freelancer who finishes client work early might experiment with creating a guide or digital resource.

A professional who saves time on research might begin writing articles or sharing insights online.

A small business owner who automates routine communication might redirect more energy toward strategy, growth, or customer relationships.

AI does not directly create these opportunities, but it can create the conditions in which they become possible.

That distinction matters.

AI is not the business.

AI is often the lever that helps a person build one.

A Shift in Perspective

Thinking of AI as a productivity multiplier changes the conversation.

Instead of asking:

Will AI replace my work?

A more useful question becomes:

How can AI amplify what I already do well?

That question leads to curiosity instead of fear.

It also points to an important truth about the future of work: the people who benefit most from AI are rarely the ones who

rely on it blindly. They are the ones who learn how to guide it, question it, and refine what it produces.
In other words, they use AI as a tool that enhances their abilities, not as a shortcut that replaces effort.
This is one of the healthiest ways to begin thinking about AI and money.
Before AI becomes a business opportunity, it often becomes a way to think more clearly, work more efficiently, and move ideas forward with less friction.
That alone can change what becomes possible.

Try This With AI

Think about a task you perform regularly in your work, business, or personal projects.

Open your preferred AI tool and ask:
"What are five ways AI could help someone in my profession work faster or more effectively?"
Then review the suggestions carefully.
Which ones seem practical?
Which ones would save time?
Which ones could improve the quality of your work?
Even small gains—saving fifteen minutes here or thirty minutes there—can add up quickly.

Reflection Question

If AI could reduce the time it takes to complete some of your regular tasks, what would you do with the extra time?
Would you take on more work?
Explore a new idea?
Experiment with a project you have been postponing?
Your answer may point toward your first real opportunity.

Starting Point #2
Curiosity as a Competitive Advantage

When people talk about success in technology, they often focus on intelligence, technical skill, or access to powerful tools. Those things can certainly help. But in moments of rapid change, another quality often matters just as much—if not more.

That quality is **curiosity**.

Curiosity is the willingness to explore something new without fully knowing where it will lead. It is the habit of asking questions, trying things, and paying attention to what happens next.

In the early stages of any technological shift, curiosity can become a powerful advantage.

Artificial intelligence is still evolving. New tools appear regularly. People are discovering new ways to use them every day. In an environment like this, no one has all the answers yet.

That means the people who benefit most are often not the ones waiting for perfect instructions. They are the ones willing to begin experimenting.

The Early Advantage

Think about other moments of technological change.

When the internet first became widely available, people who explored it early began discovering opportunities long before clear career paths existed. Some started blogs before blogging was common. Others built websites, online communities, or digital businesses.

At the time, many of those experiments probably seemed small, uncertain, or even insignificant.

But curiosity created momentum.

The same pattern is unfolding with artificial intelligence.

People who ask questions like:
What happens if I try this?
Could AI help with this task?
Is there a better way to do this with the tools now available?
often begin seeing possibilities that others overlook.

Curiosity does not guarantee success. But it does create **exposure to opportunity**.

Exploration Leads to Discovery

One of the most interesting things about AI is that its uses are not always obvious at first.

Someone might begin experimenting with AI simply out of interest—asking questions, generating ideas, or trying different prompts. During that process, they may discover that AI can help with tasks they already perform on a regular basis.

For example, someone might realize that AI can:

help outline reports
generate marketing ideas
summarize long documents
draft emails or proposals
organize research notes

At first, these discoveries may simply make work easier.

But over time, those improvements can lead to larger insights.

A freelancer might realize they can complete projects faster.

A small business owner might recognize new ways to reach customers.

A teacher might discover ways to support students more effectively.

Curiosity turns small experiments into useful discoveries.

And useful discoveries often become the foundation for new income opportunities.

Curiosity Reduces Fear

Many people approach artificial intelligence with hesitation. That reaction is understandable. Whenever a new technology begins to reshape work and communication, uncertainty follows close behind.

Curiosity offers a healthier way to respond to that uncertainty.

Instead of seeing AI only as a threat, curiosity encourages people to ask:

How does this actually work?

What can it do well?

Where does it still struggle?

These questions turn fear into learning.

The more someone interacts with AI tools, the better they understand both their strengths and their limitations. That understanding leads to better decisions about how to use them responsibly, effectively, and realistically.

In many cases, curiosity replaces anxiety with insight.

The Habit of Experimentation

Curiosity becomes most valuable when it turns into a habit. Instead of waiting for a perfect project or ideal opportunity, curious people often make experimentation part of their regular routine.

They might test a new prompt while brainstorming ideas.

They might ask AI to summarize something they are reading.

They might explore how AI handles different types of writing, planning, or problem-solving tasks.

Each small experiment adds to their understanding.

Over time, this habit builds a kind of practical expertise. Not because they memorized technical language, but because they have spent time observing what works, what does not, and where the real value seems to be.

That experience can become surprisingly valuable.

In many situations, the person who has experimented the most understands the tools far better than the person who has only read about them.

Curiosity and Opportunity

Curiosity alone does not create income. But it often leads people to the places where opportunity exists.

Imagine someone who spends a few weeks exploring how AI can help generate marketing ideas. During that process, they might notice that many small business owners struggle with exactly that problem.

Or imagine someone experimenting with AI writing tools who realizes they enjoy editing and refining the drafts AI produces. That realization could eventually turn into freelance writing, content support, or editorial services.

These opportunities rarely appear with an obvious sign that says, *Start a business here.*

They tend to emerge more gradually—as curious people explore, observe, and begin connecting ideas.

That is one reason curiosity matters so much. It helps people notice patterns before they become obvious to everyone else.

Staying Curious in a Fast-Changing Field

Artificial intelligence is developing quickly. Tools will improve. New capabilities will appear. Workflows that feel advanced today may become ordinary tomorrow.

In an environment like this, curiosity becomes a long-term advantage.

Instead of trying to master everything at once, curious people stay engaged with the process of learning. They continue asking questions, testing ideas, and adjusting as the tools evolve.

This mindset makes change less overwhelming.

Rather than trying to keep up with every development, they remain open to exploring new possibilities as they appear. Over time, that steady curiosity builds confidence.
And confidence matters, because people who feel comfortable experimenting are often the ones who spot opportunities earlier, adapt more easily, and build momentum faster.

Try This With AI
Open your preferred AI tool and ask:
"What are five interesting ways people are using AI in my profession or field?"
Review the responses and choose one idea that feels interesting, useful, or surprising.

Then ask a follow-up question:
"How could a beginner experiment with this idea?"
Even a small experiment can lead to valuable insight.

Reflection Question
When you encounter a new technology or tool, what is your first instinct?
Do you tend to wait until you fully understand it, or are you willing to explore it and learn as you go?
Curiosity often begins with a simple decision:
to look a little closer instead of turning away.

This is the second of the **33 starting points**.
The next chapter explores another powerful idea for anyone interested in making money with AI:
how to combine artificial intelligence with **skills you already have**.

Starting Point #3
Pairing AI With Skills You Already Have

When people first begin thinking about making money with artificial intelligence, they often assume they need to learn an entirely new profession.

They imagine becoming programmers, AI engineers, or technical specialists before they can benefit from the technology.

In reality, one of the most effective ways to begin is much simpler:

start with the skills you already have.

Artificial intelligence becomes most powerful when it is combined with existing knowledge, experience, or professional ability. In many cases, AI does not replace those skills—it **amplifies** them.

This is one of the most practical starting points for anyone interested in creating new opportunities with AI.

The Value You Already Bring

Every person brings a set of skills and experiences to their work.

Some people know how to write clearly.

Some understand marketing or sales.

Some are good at teaching or explaining ideas.

Others have experience organizing information, solving problems, or managing projects.

These abilities may feel ordinary because you use them regularly. But when they are paired with AI tools, they can become much more powerful.

For example:

A writer can use AI to generate ideas, outlines, and first drafts more quickly.

A marketer can use AI to brainstorm campaigns or analyze

customer feedback.

A teacher can use AI to create lesson materials or explain ideas in different ways.

A consultant can use AI to organize research and prepare reports more efficiently.

In each of these situations, AI is not replacing the person's expertise. It is helping them apply that expertise more effectively.

The human provides judgment, direction, and understanding.

The AI provides speed, structure, and support.

Together, they create something more capable than either one alone.

AI as a Tool for Extension

One useful way to think about AI is as a tool that extends your abilities.

Imagine a designer who previously needed several hours to develop ideas for a project. With the help of AI tools, that same designer might generate dozens of concepts in a fraction of the time.

Or consider someone who works in customer service. AI could help them draft responses, summarize conversations, or identify patterns in customer feedback.

In each case, the core skill still belongs to the person. AI simply expands what that skill can accomplish.

This matters because it changes how people approach opportunity.

Instead of asking, *What new career should I learn because of AI?* a more productive question becomes:

How can AI strengthen what I already know how to do?

Often, the fastest path to opportunity lies in the overlap between **existing skills and new tools**.

Finding the Intersection

To explore this idea, it helps to think about three simple categories:

Your skills — what you already know how to do

AI capabilities — what AI tools can help generate, organize, or analyze

Problems people need solved — where real demand exists

Where these three areas overlap, opportunities often begin to appear.

For example, imagine someone who enjoys writing and also understands a particular industry. AI could help them draft articles, newsletters, or reports much faster than before. Businesses in that industry might be willing to pay for that work.

Or imagine someone with a background in teaching. AI tools could help them generate lesson plans, practice questions, or educational materials. That person might turn those resources into tutoring services, study guides, workshops, or courses.

The opportunity does not come from AI alone. It comes from the **intersection between human skill and AI capability**.

Skills Become More Flexible

Another advantage of pairing AI with existing skills is flexibility.

In the past, many professional skills were tied to very specific roles or environments. Writing skills, for example, might only have been used inside a particular job or company.

AI can make those same skills more portable.

A person who understands writing, research, communication, or teaching can now apply those abilities in a wider range of ways:

helping businesses create online content

editing AI-generated drafts

creating educational resources
developing guides or digital products
Because AI reduces the time required for many tasks, people can explore more than one way of applying their skills.
Instead of relying on a single role, they can experiment with different formats, projects, services, or audiences.
That flexibility can open doors that were harder to access before.

Small Experiments Reveal Opportunities

At first, it may not be obvious how your skills and AI tools fit together.
That is where experimentation becomes valuable.
You might begin by using AI to assist with something you already do regularly. For example, you could ask AI to help outline a report, generate ideas for a project, or summarize information related to your work.
As you experiment, pay attention to moments when AI helps you complete tasks faster, more clearly, or with less effort.
Those moments often reveal where the real value lies.
Over time, small experiments may lead to bigger insights:
A task that used to take three hours now takes one.
A process that once felt difficult becomes easier.
An idea that was hard to develop suddenly has structure.
Each of these improvements points toward a possible opportunity.
What starts as a small productivity gain can eventually become a service, a product, or a new direction.

Your Experience Still Matters

One common misconception about artificial intelligence is that it removes the importance of human expertise.
In reality, the opposite is often true.

AI tools can generate information, but they do not truly understand context, nuance, priorities, or long-term consequences. That understanding comes from human experience.

Someone who has spent years working in a field brings perspective that AI alone cannot replicate. They know which ideas make sense, which ones do not, and how to shape raw information into something useful.

When AI accelerates the more mechanical parts of work—drafting, organizing, summarizing—the human expert can focus more energy on the parts that require insight, judgment, and decision-making.

That combination often produces stronger results than either one alone.

Starting Where You Are

You do not need to wait until you become an AI expert to begin exploring opportunities.

Start where you are.

Think about the skills you already use in your work, hobbies, or personal projects. Then consider how AI might help you perform those tasks faster, more creatively, or with less friction.

You may discover that the tools do not replace your abilities. They simply expand them.

And when your abilities expand, new possibilities often appear.

Try This With AI

Open your preferred AI tool and ask:

"What are five ways someone with skills in [your profession or interest] could use AI to work more efficiently or offer new services?"

Replace the bracket with your own field or skill—for example, writing, teaching, marketing, design, research, sales, or customer service.
Review the suggestions and identify one idea that seems practical, interesting, or immediately useful.

Then ask:
"What is a small experiment I could try this week to explore this idea?"

Reflection Question
What skills or knowledge do you already have that people find useful?
How might AI help you apply those abilities more efficiently—or in ways you have not considered before?
Sometimes the most promising opportunities are not entirely new.
They are simply **familiar skills applied in new ways**.

This is the third of the **33 starting points**.
The next chapter explores an idea that has become increasingly important in the age of AI:
the rise of the **one-person business**.

Starting Point #4

The Rise of the One-Person Business

For most of modern history, building a business usually required several things at once: employees, office space, significant capital, and enough time to assemble a team with different skills.

If someone had an idea, they often needed other people to help bring it to life. One person might handle writing, another marketing, another research, and another operations. Businesses grew by gathering talent and dividing responsibilities.

Artificial intelligence is beginning to change that model. Today, many individuals can build meaningful projects—and even entire businesses—with far fewer resources than before. In some cases, a single person can now accomplish work that once required a small team.

This shift has helped give rise to something increasingly common in the modern economy:

the **one-person business**.

A one-person business does not mean doing everything entirely alone. It means building something in which one person remains at the center of the operation, using tools—including AI—to expand what they can accomplish.

A Different Kind of Entrepreneurship

Traditional entrepreneurship often focused on scale.

The goal was to grow quickly, hire employees, expand operations, and increase revenue through size. That model still exists, and it will continue to matter.

But another model has quietly emerged alongside it.

Instead of building a large organization, many people are now building small, flexible businesses that serve a specific audience or solve a particular problem.

These businesses might include:
a consultant working with a handful of clients
a creator selling digital products
a writer producing newsletters or guides
a designer offering specialized services
a teacher offering courses or workshops
What makes these businesses possible is not just the internet. It is the growing ability for individuals to operate effectively without needing a large team from the beginning. Artificial intelligence accelerates that trend.

AI as a Silent Team Member

In many ways, AI functions like an invisible collaborator.
It can help brainstorm ideas, draft content, organize information, summarize research, and create first versions of projects. While it does not replace human thinking, it can assist with many of the tasks that once required additional time, effort, or personnel.

Imagine someone starting a small educational project.
They might use AI to help outline lessons, generate explanations, and summarize research. They still provide the expertise, direction, and judgment—but the drafting and organizing process becomes much faster.

Or consider someone building a consulting practice.
AI could help them analyze information, prepare reports, draft proposals, or organize client notes. The consultant still provides the strategy and insight, but the supporting work becomes easier to manage.

In cases like these, AI is not replacing a team. It is helping one person perform many roles more efficiently.

Small Businesses Can Be Powerful

One-person businesses are sometimes misunderstood.

Because they are small, people assume they must also be limited.
But size does not always determine impact.
A focused individual with the right tools can often produce valuable work, reach a global audience, and build meaningful income streams without needing a large organization behind them.
In fact, remaining small can offer real advantages.
A one-person business can adapt quickly.
It can test new ideas without layers of approval.
It can focus deeply on a specific niche or problem.
It can change direction faster when needed.
Artificial intelligence strengthens these advantages by reducing the time and effort required for many routine tasks.

Flexibility and Freedom

Another reason the one-person business model appeals to many people is flexibility.
Instead of managing large teams or complicated systems, individuals can design work around their interests, strengths, and lifestyle.
Someone might choose to work with a small number of clients they genuinely enjoy.
Another person might create digital resources that help people learn a specific skill.
Someone else might focus on teaching, writing, or sharing ideas online.
AI tools make these flexible approaches easier to support.
Tasks that once required hours of manual effort—research, drafting, organizing, summarizing—can now move faster.
That efficiency gives individuals more room to focus on creativity, relationships, problem-solving, and strategic thinking.

For many people, that is part of the appeal. They are not only trying to make money. They are trying to build a way of working that feels more intentional and more sustainable.

Starting Small Is Enough

One of the most encouraging aspects of the one-person business model is that it rarely requires a dramatic beginning.

Many successful projects start with something small:

helping a single client

publishing a helpful article

creating a simple guide or resource

sharing useful insights online

These small steps often grow into something larger over time.

Artificial intelligence can support this process by lowering the barriers to experimentation. When drafting, organizing, and researching become easier, individuals can test ideas more quickly and learn what works.

Progress becomes less about waiting for the perfect plan and more about **taking small steps and paying attention to the results**.

That mindset matters.

Many people never begin because they assume a business has to start as something polished, complete, and fully formed. But in reality, many businesses begin as simple acts of usefulness repeated consistently.

Designing Work Intentionally

The rise of the one-person business also invites a different way of thinking about work.

Instead of asking, *How big can this become?* people sometimes ask:

What kind of work do I want to build?
Who do I want to help?
What problems am I interested in solving?
These are important questions, because not every meaningful business needs to become large.
Some people want a business that gives them freedom.
Some want a business that supports creative expression.
Some want a business that fits alongside other priorities in life.
AI tools make it easier for individuals to explore these questions because they reduce the friction involved in testing ideas.
A person can experiment with writing, teaching, consulting, or creating resources without needing a large infrastructure.
Over time, those experiments may grow into something sustainable.

AI Does Not Replace the Person
It is important to remember that AI does not replace the individual at the center of a one-person business.
It cannot define the purpose of the work.
It cannot build trust with clients or audiences.
It cannot understand the deeper motivations behind a project.
It cannot decide what kind of business is worth building.
Those elements still come from the person.
AI can assist with the mechanics of work, but meaning, creativity, trust, and direction still come from human intention.
That is why the most successful one-person businesses tend to combine two things:
human insight and AI-supported efficiency.
AI may help a person move faster, but it is still the person who decides where they are going.

Try This With AI
Ask your AI tool:
"What are five types of small businesses a single person could start using AI tools?"
Review the suggestions and notice which ones align with your interests, existing skills, or life experience.

Then ask a follow-up question:
"What would be the simplest version of this idea that someone could start with?"
Often the most useful ideas begin in small, manageable forms.

Reflection Question
If you could build a small business around your skills, interests, or experience, what problem would you most enjoy helping people solve?
Sometimes the path toward meaningful work does not begin with building something large.
It begins with building something **focused, useful, and human**.

This is the fourth of the **33 starting points**.
The next chapter explores another idea that often leads to opportunity in the age of AI:
why **small problems can lead to surprisingly valuable solutions**.

Starting Point #5
AI Writing Services

Difficulty: Beginner
Startup Cost: Low
Time to First Income: 1–2 weeks
Income Type: Service-based

What It Is

One of the fastest ways to start making money with AI is by offering **AI-assisted writing services**.

Businesses constantly need written content. They need blog posts, website pages, social media captions, product descriptions, newsletters, and marketing materials. For many business owners, creating this content takes time they simply do not have.

Artificial intelligence makes the drafting and organizing process much faster. While AI can generate an initial version of the text, the real value comes from the human who edits, shapes, and improves it.

In this model, AI helps produce the **first draft**, while the person offering the service refines the message, adjusts the tone, and ensures the writing fits the client's goals.

The result is a service that combines the speed of AI with the judgment and communication skills of a human editor.

For many people, this is one of the easiest and most accessible entry points into earning money with AI.

Why This Works Now

Content has become essential for almost every business.

Companies need written material for:

- websites
- blogs
- newsletters

- social media posts
- product descriptions
- advertisements

But creating consistent content takes time, and many small business owners struggle to keep up with it.

AI dramatically speeds up the early stages of writing. It can help generate outlines, brainstorm ideas, and produce first drafts in minutes rather than hours.

That efficiency creates an opportunity for individuals who can guide the process and deliver polished, ready-to-use content.

Businesses are not paying for the AI itself. They are paying for someone who can:

- understand their message
- organize ideas clearly
- refine and edit the output
- deliver useful, publishable content

AI simply makes it easier to provide that service quickly and efficiently.

Who This Is Best For

This starting point works especially well for people who:

- enjoy writing or editing
- are comfortable organizing ideas
- communicate clearly
- understand how businesses talk to customers

You do not need to be a professional writer to begin. Many successful writing services focus on **clear, helpful communication**, not literary perfection.

If you can explain ideas clearly, adjust tone for different audiences, and review AI-generated drafts carefully, this can become a valuable service.

What You Need

The basic setup is simple.
You need:

- one AI writing tool
- a basic document editor
- a way to communicate with clients

You may also want to create a simple portfolio showing examples of writing you can produce.
These examples do not have to come from paid clients. You can create sample blog posts, newsletters, or product descriptions to demonstrate your ability.
The key is showing that you can turn AI-generated drafts into **clear, useful content**.

How to Start in 24 Hours
The easiest way to begin is by focusing on a specific type of content.
Step 1: Choose a content type
Examples include blog posts, email newsletters, product descriptions, or social media captions.
Step 2: Create two or three sample pieces
Use AI to generate a first draft, then edit it carefully so it reads naturally and clearly.
Step 3: Identify a niche
Examples include local restaurants, fitness coaches, real estate agents, or small online stores.
Step 4: Write a simple service offer
Example:
"AI-assisted blog writing for small businesses."
Step 5: Reach out to potential clients
Contact small businesses directly, post your offer online, or list your service on freelance marketplaces.
The goal is not to build a large business immediately. The goal is to gain experience and complete your **first project**.

How to Make Your First $100

A simple starting offer could look like this:

“Five social media captions for your business — $25.”

If you sell that package to four clients, you have made your first $100.

Another option could be:

“One blog post (800 words) — $50.”

Two clients would reach the same milestone.

The exact price matters less than the experience of completing real work and delivering value to someone.

Once you complete a few projects, you can begin increasing prices or offering larger packages.

How to Grow It

If this starting point works well for you, there are several ways it can grow.

You might:

- offer monthly content packages
- specialize in a particular industry
- provide newsletter writing or email marketing support
- add content planning or editing services

Over time, some people expand writing services into agencies or combine them with digital products such as templates, guides, or writing frameworks.

But the important part is the beginning.

Most successful service businesses start with **one client, one project, and one useful result**.

Watch-Outs

There are a few common mistakes to avoid when offering AI-assisted writing services.

First, do not rely entirely on AI output without reviewing it carefully. AI-generated text often requires editing to ensure it is accurate, clear, and appropriate for the audience.
Second, avoid presenting AI-generated work as fully original writing without transparency when necessary. Ethical use of AI builds long-term trust with clients.
Finally, remember that the value you provide is not the AI tool itself. It is your ability to guide the process and deliver content that genuinely helps the client communicate.

Try This Next
Ask your AI tool:
"Create an outline for a blog post that helps small businesses understand the benefits of using AI for marketing."
Then review the outline and expand it into a short article.
Edit the draft carefully so it reads naturally and clearly.
This exercise will help you practice the same workflow used in many AI-assisted writing services.

Reflection Question
What type of writing feels most natural or enjoyable for you? Blog posts, emails, product descriptions, and social media content all serve different purposes. Identifying the type of writing that suits you best can help you focus your efforts and build confidence more quickly.
Sometimes the easiest opportunities begin with a simple skill you already use every day.

This is the fifth of the **33 starting points**.
The next chapter explores another opportunity that has become increasingly popular in the AI economy:

creating AI-assisted social media content for businesses.

Starting Point #6
AI Social Media Content Creation

Difficulty: Beginner
Startup Cost: Low
Time to First Income: 1–2 weeks
Income Type: Service-based

What It Is
Another practical way to begin earning money with AI is by helping businesses create **social media content**.
Most businesses understand that they should maintain an active presence on platforms such as Instagram, Facebook, LinkedIn, or TikTok. Regular posting helps them stay visible, build trust with customers, and attract new business.
The problem is consistency.
Many business owners run out of ideas, struggle to find time to write posts, or simply feel unsure about what to share. As a result, their social media presence becomes irregular or neglected.
AI tools can help solve that problem.
They can generate content ideas, draft captions, suggest themes, and help organize posting schedules. When combined with human editing and judgment, this becomes a valuable service for businesses that want help showing up consistently online.
In this model, AI helps with brainstorming and drafting, while you organize, refine, and deliver finished content the business can actually use.

Why This Works Now
Social media has become one of the most common ways businesses connect with customers.

Restaurants share new menu items.
Fitness coaches post workout tips.
Real estate agents highlight listings.
Local shops showcase promotions or featured products.
But many small businesses struggle to keep up. They may post frequently for a few weeks, then disappear for months because they run out of time, energy, or ideas.
AI makes it easier to maintain a steady flow of content.
With AI, someone can quickly generate:

- caption ideas
- content themes
- short post drafts
- engagement questions
- promotional messages

Instead of spending hours trying to decide what to post, the first round of ideas appears quickly. The person providing the service can then refine those ideas so they match the business's tone, audience, and goals.
Businesses benefit because they receive consistent, organized content. The service provider benefits because AI helps make that work more efficient.

Who This Is Best For

This starting point works well for people who:

- enjoy social media
- understand how businesses communicate with customers
- can organize ideas into short, clear posts
- have a feel for tone, voice, and audience

You do not need to be a marketing expert to begin. Many businesses simply need someone who can help them post consistently and communicate clearly.

If you can combine basic social media understanding with AI-assisted drafting, this can become a useful and approachable service.

What You Need

The setup is simple.

You need:

- one AI writing tool
- a document, spreadsheet, or content calendar to organize posts
- a way to communicate with clients

Some people also use design tools to create simple graphics or lay out content calendars, but that is optional at the beginning.

What matters most is your ability to deliver **clear, organized content** that businesses can easily review and post.

How to Start in 24 Hours

The easiest way to begin is by creating a simple **social media content package**.

Step 1: Choose one platform

Start with one platform such as Instagram, Facebook, or LinkedIn. It is easier to build confidence when you focus on one format first.

Step 2: Create a sample content set

Use AI to generate 10–15 caption ideas for a specific type of business.

Example:

"Instagram captions for a local coffee shop."

Step 3: Edit and refine the captions

Make sure they sound natural, useful, and appropriate for a real business.

Step 4: Create a simple service offer
Example:
"12 social media captions for your business each month."
Step 5: Reach out to potential clients
Contact small businesses in your area, message businesses online, or post your service on freelance platforms.
The goal is not to build an agency overnight. The goal is to land your **first paying client** and gain real experience.

How to Make Your First $100
A simple starter offer might look like this:
"10 social media captions for your business — $25."
If you sell that package to four clients, you have made your first $100.
Another option could be:
"One month of captions (12 posts) — $75."
Just two clients would put you past your first $100.
As you gain experience, many providers move toward **monthly packages**, which can create recurring income.
For example:

- $150 per month for 12 posts
- $300 per month for 20 posts
- $500+ per month for fuller content support

The exact pricing will vary by niche, quality, and scope. What matters most at the beginning is proving that you can create useful content consistently.

How to Grow It
If you enjoy this kind of work, there are several ways it can grow.
You might:

- specialize in one industry, such as restaurants, fitness, or real estate
- create monthly content calendars

- offer caption writing plus post ideas or image suggestions
- help businesses plan promotions or seasonal campaigns

Over time, some people combine social media content creation with related services such as newsletter writing, blog posts, or marketing support.

Others turn their systems into digital products, such as content templates, caption packs, or niche-specific planning kits.

The starting point remains simple: helping businesses stay visible and consistent online.

Watch-Outs

One common mistake is relying too heavily on AI-generated captions without editing them.

Social media works best when posts feel human, relevant, and aligned with the business's personality. AI can help generate ideas, but the final message should still sound like the business, not like a machine.

Another challenge is trying to serve too many platforms at once. It is usually easier to start with one platform, one type of business, and one simple offer.

Finally, remember that the real value you provide is not the AI tool itself. It is your ability to organize ideas, create consistency, and help businesses communicate clearly with their audience.

Try This Next

Ask your AI tool:

"Generate 15 Instagram caption ideas for a small local coffee shop trying to attract more morning customers."

Review the results and choose the five strongest captions.

Then edit them so they feel more natural, more specific, and more engaging.
This exercise will help you practice the exact workflow used in AI-assisted social media services.

Reflection Question
Think about the types of businesses you notice in your area or online.
Which ones seem inconsistent on social media, even though they clearly have something worth promoting?
Those businesses may represent your first potential clients.

This is the sixth of the **33 starting points**.
The next chapter explores another valuable opportunity created by AI:
using AI to assist with research and information gathering for professionals and businesses.

Starting Point #7
AI Research Assistance

Difficulty: Beginner to Intermediate
Startup Cost: Low
Time to First Income: 1–3 weeks
Income Type: Service-based

What It Is

Another valuable way to earn money with AI is by helping professionals and businesses **gather, organize, and summarize information**.

Many people need research to do their work effectively. Consultants research industries. Writers gather background information for articles. Business owners study competitors. Students and educators explore complex topics.

The challenge is that research takes time.

Searching through articles, reports, websites, and documents often requires hours of reading, sorting, and organizing before useful insights begin to emerge.

AI tools can dramatically speed up that process.

They can help identify relevant information, summarize long documents, spot patterns, and organize ideas into notes or reports. When combined with careful human review, this creates an opportunity to provide **AI-assisted research services**.

In this model, AI helps process large amounts of information quickly, while the human ensures accuracy, clarity, and usefulness.

Why This Works Now

Information has never been more abundant.

Businesses and professionals constantly need to understand markets, trends, competitors, technologies, and customer behavior. But sorting through that volume of information can feel overwhelming.

AI tools make it easier to scan, summarize, and organize information quickly.

For example, AI can help:

- summarize long articles or reports
- compare multiple sources
- extract key insights from documents
- organize research notes into structured summaries
- generate outlines based on collected information

Instead of spending hours reading dozens of sources from scratch, someone can use AI to create a strong starting point and then refine the results.

That efficiency creates a service opportunity for people who can combine AI assistance with careful review and clear presentation.

Professionals often value **well-organized information**, especially when it saves them time and helps them make decisions faster.

Who This Is Best For

This starting point works well for people who:

- enjoy learning about new topics
- are comfortable reading and summarizing information
- have strong attention to detail
- like organizing ideas into clear formats

It can also be a strong fit for people with experience in writing, consulting, education, project management, or strategy work.

You do not need to be a technical expert to begin. What matters most is your ability to turn scattered information into something useful, accurate, and easy to understand.

What You Need

The setup is straightforward.

You need:

- an AI research or writing tool
- access to online information sources
- a document editor to organize your findings
- a way to communicate with clients

Some projects may also involve spreadsheets, short reports, or structured summaries.

The key skill is learning how to guide AI tools effectively while carefully reviewing the information they produce.

In this kind of work, **accuracy and clarity matter a great deal**.

How to Start in 24 Hours

You can begin exploring this opportunity by practicing a simple research task.

Step 1: Choose a topic

Select a subject that a business or professional might care about.

Example:

"Local coffee shop market trends."

Step 2: Use AI to gather initial insights

Ask AI to summarize trends, challenges, or opportunities related to the topic.

Step 3: Verify and expand the information

Check the information against credible sources and improve the summary so it is accurate and clear.

Step 4: Turn the information into a short report
Create a one-page or two-page summary with key insights and bullet points.
Step 5: Identify people who might need research help
Consultants, small business owners, content creators, educators, and students often need support gathering and organizing information.
Your goal is to practice producing **clear, useful summaries** that save other people time.

How to Make Your First $100

A simple way to begin is by offering **small research tasks**.
For example:

- a one-page summary of industry trends — $50
- a competitor research summary — $50
- topic research for an article, presentation, or proposal — $25 to $75

Two small projects could easily take you to your first $100.
Many clients are willing to pay for research if it saves them several hours of work or helps them organize information more effectively.
Once you build confidence, you can move into larger reports, recurring research support, or niche-specific services.

How to Grow It

If you enjoy research work, this opportunity can grow in several directions.
You might:

- specialize in research for a specific industry
- assist writers or creators with background research
- provide competitor analysis for small businesses

- create structured reports for consultants or agencies

Some people also combine research services with writing, editing, strategy, or content planning.
Over time, research expertise can become a valuable part of a broader consulting or knowledge-based business.
The more clearly you organize and communicate information, the more valuable your work becomes.

Watch-Outs

One important caution is that AI-generated summaries are not always fully accurate.
AI tools can misunderstand information, miss context, or produce statements that need verification.
Because of this, careful review is essential.
Always check sources when accuracy matters, especially in professional, academic, or business settings.
Another common mistake is delivering too much raw information instead of clear insights.
Clients usually want **clarity**, not a pile of notes or data. The value of your service comes from turning complex information into something organized, understandable, and useful.

Try This Next

Ask your AI tool:
"Summarize the three biggest trends affecting small retail businesses in the next five years."
Then review the results and organize them into a short one-page summary with bullet points.
Focus on making the information clear, structured, and useful.
This is exactly the kind of task many professionals would appreciate having help with.

Reflection Question
Think about the topics you naturally enjoy learning about. Markets, technology, health, education, finance, travel, and many other areas constantly require research.
Which of these areas might you enjoy exploring and summarizing for others?
Sometimes the path to useful work begins with curiosity and the ability to explain what you learn clearly.

This is the seventh of the **33 starting points**.
The next chapter explores another practical opportunity created by AI:
helping local businesses understand and adopt AI tools.

Starting Point #8
Helping Local Businesses Use AI

Difficulty: Beginner to Intermediate
Startup Cost: Low
Time to First Income: 2–4 weeks
Income Type: Service-based

What It Is

Another growing opportunity is helping **local businesses understand and use AI tools in practical ways**.

Many small business owners have heard about artificial intelligence. They see headlines about AI transforming industries, automating tasks, and improving productivity. But for many of them, the technology still feels confusing, abstract, or intimidating.

They may wonder:

What tools should I use?

How could this actually help my business?

Is this something I should be paying attention to right now?

Most small business owners do not have the time to research these questions in depth. They are busy running day-to-day operations.

That creates an opportunity for someone who understands AI tools to act as a **guide, teacher, or advisor**.

In this role, you help businesses identify simple ways AI can save time, improve communication, and support marketing or operations.

You are not selling complicated technology.

You are helping business owners apply AI in ways that feel **practical, approachable, and useful**.

Why This Works Now

Artificial intelligence is advancing quickly, but adoption among small businesses is still uneven.

Large companies often have technology teams exploring new tools. Small businesses usually do not.

Many local businesses still rely on manual processes for tasks such as:

- writing marketing content
- responding to customer messages
- organizing notes or documents
- brainstorming promotional ideas
- conducting basic research

AI tools can assist with many of these tasks, often saving meaningful time.

However, the biggest barrier for many business owners is not access to the tools. It is understanding **how to use them effectively and where they actually fit into the business**.

Someone who can explain AI clearly, demonstrate simple workflows, and help implement small improvements can provide real value.

In many cases, businesses are willing to pay for guidance that saves time, reduces friction, or improves efficiency.

Who This Is Best For

This starting point works well for people who:

- enjoy learning about technology
- can explain ideas clearly to others
- have patience when teaching or demonstrating tools
- are comfortable experimenting with new workflows

You do not need to be a software engineer or AI developer.

In many cases, the most valuable skill is the ability to **translate complex technology into simple, practical use cases**.

If you can show a business owner how AI might help them write marketing content faster, organize ideas, or generate new promotions, that guidance can be very valuable.

What You Need

The setup for this type of work is simple.

You need:

- familiarity with a few AI tools
- the ability to demonstrate basic workflows
- a way to communicate with business owners
- simple documents or examples that explain how the tools work

You may also want to create short guides, demonstrations, or step-by-step instructions that businesses can follow after your session.

The most important asset is your ability to make AI feel **approachable and useful**, rather than technical or overwhelming.

How to Start in 24 Hours

You can begin exploring this opportunity by identifying a few practical business use cases.

Step 1: Learn a few simple AI workflows

Examples might include:

- generating marketing ideas
- drafting customer responses
- brainstorming social media content
- summarizing information or reports

Step 2: Create a short demonstration

Write a simple example showing how AI can save time for a specific type of business.

Example:

"Using AI to create weekly social media captions for a local restaurant."

Step 3: Identify businesses that might benefit
Local businesses, consultants, service providers, and small teams often appreciate practical productivity tools.
Step 4: Offer a simple introduction session
For example:
"A one-hour introduction to practical AI tools for small businesses."
Step 5: Demonstrate real examples
During the session, show how the tools can help with everyday tasks the business already handles.
Your goal is to help business owners leave with **one or two workflows they can use immediately**.

How to Make Your First $100

A simple starting offer could be:
"AI Basics for Small Businesses — One-hour session."
You might charge $50 for an introductory session with one business owner.
Two sessions would take you to your first $100.
Another option is offering a small workshop for multiple business owners.
For example:
"AI Productivity Workshop for Local Businesses — $25 per attendee."
With five participants, you would reach $125.
As you gain experience, you may begin offering higher-value services such as workflow setup, staff training, or ongoing consulting.

How to Grow It

If you enjoy helping businesses adopt AI, this opportunity can grow in several directions.
You might:

- provide training sessions for small teams

- help businesses set up simple AI workflows
- create guides or templates for common tasks
- offer ongoing consulting or productivity coaching

Some people also create educational content, workshops, or courses focused on practical AI use within specific industries.

Over time, this type of work can evolve into **AI consulting, small business advisory services, or niche training programs**.

The key is starting with simple, useful guidance that helps businesses solve everyday problems.

Watch-Outs

One common mistake is overwhelming business owners with too many tools or overly technical explanations.

Most small business owners are not looking for advanced systems. They want **simple solutions that save time and improve their daily work**.

Focus on practical workflows rather than complicated technology.

Another important point is setting realistic expectations. AI tools can be extremely helpful, but they are not perfect and still require human judgment.

Helping businesses understand both the strengths and limitations of AI builds trust and credibility.

Try This Next

Ask your AI tool:

"List five ways a local restaurant could use AI to save time on marketing and customer communication."

Review the suggestions and choose the two most practical ideas.

Then write a short explanation of how those workflows might work in a real business.
This exercise helps you practice identifying **practical AI use cases**, which is the core skill behind this opportunity.

Reflection Question
Think about the businesses you interact with regularly. Which of them seem curious about new technology but unsure how to use it?
Helping those businesses understand and apply AI tools may become one of the most practical ways to create value in the coming years.

This is the eighth of the **33 starting points**.
The next chapter explores another powerful opportunity created by AI:
creating digital products that can be sold online.

Starting Point #9

Creating Digital Products With AI

Difficulty: Beginner to Intermediate
Startup Cost: Low
Time to First Income: 2–6 weeks
Income Type: Product-based

What It Is

Another powerful opportunity created by AI is the ability to **create digital products that can be sold online**.

A digital product is something useful that people can download, access, or use without requiring physical shipping. Examples include guides, templates, worksheets, prompt packs, planners, toolkits, and instructional resources.

In the past, creating these kinds of products often required significant time. Writing guides, organizing templates, designing worksheets, or developing instructional materials could take weeks or even months.

AI tools now make it much easier to brainstorm ideas, structure content, generate outlines, and organize information.

The result is that individuals can create useful digital products more quickly and test different ideas at a much lower cost.

In this model, AI helps generate early drafts and structure, while the human organizes, edits, and shapes the final product into something genuinely useful.

Why This Works Now

More people are searching online for resources that help them solve specific problems.

Someone may want:

- a budgeting template

- a fitness planner
- a business checklist
- a content calendar
- a study guide
- a set of prompts or worksheets

Digital products are appealing because they are usually affordable, easy to access, and immediately useful.

AI helps accelerate the creation process. It can assist with brainstorming product ideas, outlining content, drafting explanations, and organizing materials into a usable format. This allows creators to spend less time staring at a blank page and more time refining and improving what they make.

Unlike service work, digital products also have the potential to be sold repeatedly. Once created, the same product can be sold to many different customers.

That does not make the income effortless, but it does make it more scalable.

Who This Is Best For

This starting point works well for people who:

- enjoy organizing ideas into useful resources
- like creating guides, templates, or educational materials
- have knowledge or experience in a particular topic
- are interested in building something that can be sold more than once

You do not need to be an expert in every field to create a useful product. Many successful digital products focus on **simple, practical solutions** to common problems.

If you can identify a problem people face and create a resource that helps solve it, that product may have value.

What You Need

The setup for creating digital products is relatively simple. You need:

- an AI writing or brainstorming tool
- a way to design or organize the product, such as documents, templates, or design tools
- a platform where the product can be sold or shared
- a basic understanding of the audience you want to help

Many digital products begin as simple documents or templates. As you gain experience, you may explore more advanced formats such as structured guides, interactive worksheets, or bundled resources.
The most important element is usefulness.
A simple product that solves a clear problem can often be more valuable than a more complex product with no clear purpose.

How to Start in 24 Hours

You can begin exploring digital products by focusing on a small, specific idea.

Step 1: Identify a problem people face

Think about tasks people often struggle with or want help organizing.
Examples might include:

- planning social media content
- tracking personal habits
- organizing study notes
- managing small business tasks

Step 2: Ask AI for product ideas

Use AI to brainstorm possible templates, checklists, or guides related to that problem.

Step 3: Choose one simple product idea

Focus on something small and useful.

Example:
"A weekly content planner for small business owners."
Step 4: Use AI to help outline the product
Generate sections, explanations, prompts, or structure that make the resource more useful.
Step 5: Design the final version
Organize the information into a clean, clear format that people can easily understand and use.
The goal is not to create the perfect product. The goal is to create something useful and test whether people find it helpful.

How to Make Your First $100
A simple digital product might sell for $5 to $20, depending on the audience and the value it provides.
For example:

- a $10 template sold 10 times = $100
- a $20 planner sold 5 times = $100

Digital marketplaces, personal websites, and creator platforms can all be places where these products are sold.
At the beginning, your goal is not massive scale. Your goal is learning which types of products people actually want.
Each product you create teaches you more about your audience and the kinds of problems they care about solving.

How to Grow It
If you enjoy creating digital products, there are many ways to expand.
You might:

- create bundles of related products
- develop niche resources for specific audiences
- turn templates into larger guides or toolkits
- build collections of prompts or frameworks

Some creators also combine digital products with services, courses, or educational content.
Over time, a collection of useful resources can become a small library of products that generates ongoing income.
The key is focusing on **clarity and usefulness** rather than complexity.

Watch-Outs
One common mistake is creating products that are too broad or vague.
Digital products usually work best when they solve a **specific problem**.
For example, “Productivity planner” is broad.
“Weekly planner for freelance designers managing multiple clients” is much more specific.
Another challenge is relying too heavily on AI-generated content without refining it. AI can help structure ideas, but the final product should still feel thoughtful, organized, and easy to use.
Your role is to transform rough ideas into something practical and polished.

Try This Next
Ask your AI tool:
“List five simple digital products that could help small business owners organize their weekly marketing tasks.”
Review the suggestions and choose one idea.
Then ask AI to help outline the sections or structure of that product.
This exercise will help you practice the process of turning ideas into simple digital resources.

Reflection Question

Think about tasks you organize regularly in your own life or work.
What templates, checklists, or guides might make those tasks easier for someone else?
Sometimes the best digital products come from solving problems you already understand.

This is the ninth of the **33 starting points**.
The next chapter explores another opportunity created by AI: **using AI to support freelancers and independent professionals in delivering their services more efficiently.**

Starting Point #10
AI for Freelancers

Difficulty: Beginner to Intermediate
Startup Cost: Low
Time to First Income: Immediate to 2 weeks
Income Type: Service-based

What It Is

Another practical way to make money with AI is by using it to **improve the services you already offer as a freelancer**. Freelancers work in many fields, including writing, design, marketing, consulting, editing, research, virtual assistance, and project management. In these areas, much of the work involves organizing information, generating ideas, communicating clearly, and delivering results efficiently.
AI tools can assist with many of these tasks.
Rather than replacing freelance work, AI often acts as a **productivity partner**. It can help generate ideas, draft content, organize research, and streamline repetitive tasks. This allows freelancers to complete projects more efficiently, take on additional clients, or improve the quality of their deliverables.
In many cases, the opportunity is not about creating an entirely new business. It is about **enhancing the value and efficiency of work you already know how to do.**

Why This Works Now

Freelancers often face a common challenge: balancing time and income.
Because freelancers typically charge per project or per hour, their earning potential is often limited by how much work they can complete within a certain amount of time.
AI can shift that balance.

By assisting with brainstorming, outlining, drafting, summarizing, and organizing information, AI tools can reduce the time required for many common freelance tasks. For example, AI can help freelancers:

- generate ideas for marketing campaigns
- draft outlines for articles or presentations
- summarize research materials
- organize notes or meeting transcripts
- create first drafts of written content

This does not eliminate the freelancer's role. The freelancer still provides judgment, expertise, editing, and final quality control.

But by reducing the time spent on early-stage work, freelancers can focus more on refining and delivering high-quality results.

Who This Is Best For

This starting point works well for people who already provide freelance services or are considering doing so.

Examples include:

- writers and editors
- designers and content creators
- marketers and social media managers
- consultants and strategists
- virtual assistants
- researchers or analysts

If your work involves creating, organizing, or communicating information, AI can likely assist with part of the process.

Freelancers who learn how to integrate AI into their workflows often gain an advantage because they can deliver results **more quickly and consistently**.

What You Need

The setup for AI-assisted freelance work is simple.

You need:

- one or more AI tools that support your workflow
- a clear understanding of the services you provide
- a system for reviewing and refining AI-generated output
- a way to communicate with clients and deliver finished work

You may also want to experiment with prompts or workflows that help you consistently generate useful drafts or ideas. The key is learning how AI fits into your existing process rather than trying to replace the process entirely.

How to Start in 24 Hours

If you already provide freelance services, the easiest way to begin is by identifying where AI might save time in your current workflow.

Step 1: Identify repetitive tasks

Think about parts of your work that take time but follow a similar pattern each time.

Examples might include:

- drafting outlines
- summarizing research
- generating content ideas
- organizing notes

Step 2: Ask AI to assist

Experiment with prompts that help AI generate drafts or structure your ideas.

Step 3: Refine the results

Review the output carefully and edit it to match the quality your clients expect.

Step 4: Track time saved

Notice how much faster certain tasks become when AI assists with the early stages.

Step 5: Adjust your workflow

Incorporate AI where it helps and continue refining your process.

Even small improvements in efficiency can make a meaningful difference over time.

How to Make Your First $100

For many freelancers, AI can increase income simply by improving efficiency.

If AI helps reduce the time required to complete a project, you may be able to:

- complete additional projects
- offer faster turnaround times
- add new services to your offerings

For example, a freelance writer who previously completed two articles per week might be able to complete three or four using AI-assisted outlining and drafting.

A social media manager might add content planning services with the help of AI-generated ideas.

Even one additional project could easily represent an extra $100 or more.

How to Grow It

As freelancers become more comfortable using AI, they often discover ways to expand their services.

You might:

- add service packages that include AI-assisted research or content creation
- offer faster turnaround times for clients
- specialize in a niche where AI significantly improves your workflow

- develop systems that allow you to handle larger or more complex projects

Some freelancers also turn their workflows into **templates, guides, or digital products** that help others perform similar work.

Over time, AI can become a powerful tool for improving both productivity and profitability.

Watch-Outs

One important mistake to avoid is relying too heavily on AI without reviewing the results.

Clients expect accuracy, clarity, and professionalism. AI-generated content should always be reviewed, edited, and improved before delivery.

Another consideration is transparency.

Some clients may want to know whether AI tools are used during the process. Being open about how AI assists your workflow can help maintain trust.

Finally, remember that AI is most valuable when it supports your expertise rather than replacing it.

Your judgment, creativity, and understanding of client needs are still what make your work valuable.

Try This Next

Ask your AI tool:

"What are five ways a freelance [writer / designer / marketer / consultant] could use AI to improve their workflow?"

Replace the bracket with your field.

Review the suggestions and test one idea during your next project.

This simple experiment may reveal ways to save time or improve your process.

Reflection Question

Think about the services you currently offer or might offer as a freelancer.

Which parts of that work take the most time?

Learning how AI can assist with those tasks may open the door to higher productivity and increased income.

This is the tenth of the **33 starting points**.

The next chapter explores another opportunity created by AI: **creative work such as art, writing, and media production.**

Starting Point #11
AI-Assisted Creative Work

Difficulty: Beginner to Intermediate
Startup Cost: Low to Medium
Time to First Income: 2–4 weeks
Income Type: Service-based or Product-based

What It Is

Another growing opportunity in the AI economy is using AI to support **creative work**.

Creative professionals produce things such as artwork, illustrations, designs, videos, music, written content, and multimedia experiences. This kind of work usually requires both imagination and time.

AI tools can assist with many stages of the creative process. They can help generate visual concepts, brainstorm story ideas, produce drafts, suggest variations, and help creators explore styles or directions they might not have considered on their own.

In this model, AI does not replace the creator. Instead, it acts as a tool that helps speed up exploration, iteration, and production.

The human creator still makes the key decisions: choosing ideas, refining the output, shaping the final result, and making sure the work connects with an audience.

For many people, AI-assisted creativity opens the door to producing work more quickly and experimenting with new types of projects.

Why This Works Now

Creative industries constantly need new content.
Businesses need graphics for marketing. Social media creators need images and videos. Authors and educators

need illustrations and visual explanations. Content creators often need thumbnails, covers, and design assets.

At the same time, tools for producing creative work have historically required significant training, time, or expensive software.

AI tools have lowered that barrier.

Today, people can generate visual concepts, draft scripts, explore artistic directions, and create design elements much faster than before.

This shift allows individuals who may not have traditional design training to participate in creative markets. It also helps experienced creatives work more efficiently.

In both cases, AI expands the range of what one person can produce.

Who This Is Best For

This starting point works well for people who enjoy creative work or visual communication.

Examples include:

- artists and illustrators
- designers and visual creators
- video editors and media creators
- writers and storytellers
- content creators and social media producers

It can also be a strong fit for people who enjoy experimenting with ideas and exploring different creative styles.

You do not need to master every creative discipline. Many creators focus on one type of output, such as graphics, short videos, illustrations, or digital artwork.

The key is learning how to combine AI-generated ideas with **human taste, editing, and refinement**.

What You Need

The setup for AI-assisted creative work depends on the type of content you want to produce.
In most cases, you need:

- one or more AI creative tools
- a basic editing or design platform
- a place to share or sell your work
- time to experiment with styles and ideas

You may also benefit from studying examples of successful work in the area you want to explore.
Understanding what audiences respond to can help guide the type of work you produce.

How to Start in 24 Hours

You can begin exploring AI-assisted creative work by experimenting with a small project.

Step 1: Choose a creative format

Examples include:

- digital illustrations
- short videos
- social media graphics
- story concepts
- design elements

Step 2: Use AI to generate initial ideas

Ask AI to suggest concepts, styles, or creative directions.

Step 3: Create sample content

Generate several examples using AI tools.

Step 4: Refine the best results

Edit the strongest outputs so they look polished, consistent, and intentional.

Step 5: Share or test your work

Post examples online, show them to potential clients, or create a simple portfolio.

The goal is not perfection. The goal is discovering what type of creative work you enjoy producing and where your skills may have market value.

How to Make Your First $100

There are several ways AI-assisted creative work can generate early income.

You might:

- create graphics for small businesses
- design social media visuals
- sell digital artwork online
- produce thumbnails or cover images for creators
- offer simple design services to local businesses

For example:

A creator might design social media graphics for $25 per set. Completing four small projects would take you to your first $100.

Another option is selling digital artwork, design assets, or themed visual packs through online marketplaces.

The key is starting with small, practical projects that help you build experience and identify what people are willing to pay for.

How to Grow It

If you enjoy creative work, this opportunity can grow in several directions.

You might:

- specialize in a particular style or niche
- build a portfolio for a specific industry
- sell digital art, design assets, or templates
- collaborate with businesses or creators who need visual content

Some creators also combine AI-assisted art with other opportunities such as digital products, educational content, branding services, or media production.
Over time, a recognizable style and a consistent portfolio can attract clients, customers, or audiences who appreciate your work.

Watch-Outs
One challenge with AI-assisted creative work is that the initial output often requires refinement.
Raw AI outputs may look interesting, but they usually still need editing, adjustment, or improvement before they become polished pieces.
Another important consideration is originality and ethical use.
Creators should pay attention to licensing rules, usage rights, and platform guidelines when using AI tools for commercial work.
Your value as a creator does not come simply from generating images or ideas.
It comes from your ability to guide the creative process, make strong choices, and shape the final result into something worth using, sharing, or buying.

Try This Next
Ask your AI tool:
"Generate five creative project ideas that combine AI tools with digital art or media."
Choose one idea and create a small sample project.
This simple exercise will help you explore how AI can support creative production and what kind of work you may want to develop further.

Reflection Question
Think about the kinds of creative work you naturally enjoy.

Is it visual design, storytelling, video production, illustration, or another form of expression?
AI can open new doors for creative experimentation. The key is finding the type of work that feels both enjoyable to make and valuable to others.

This is the eleventh of the **33 starting points**.
The next chapter explores another opportunity created by AI: **using AI to build niche content websites and information resources.**

Starting Point #12

Building Niche Content Websites With AI

Difficulty: Beginner to Intermediate
Startup Cost: Low
Time to First Income: 1–3 months
Income Type: Product-based or Advertising-based

What It Is

Another opportunity created by AI is building **niche content websites** that focus on a specific topic or audience.

A niche website is a site that provides helpful information about a particular subject. These websites often focus on answering common questions, explaining ideas clearly, or sharing useful resources related to topics people are searching for online.

Examples might include websites about:

- personal budgeting
- pet care
- fitness training
- travel planning
- home improvement
- technology tools

In the past, creating large amounts of website content required significant time and effort. Researching topics, outlining articles, and writing explanations often took hours for each piece of content.

AI tools can now assist with many parts of that process. They can help brainstorm article ideas, organize outlines, summarize information, and generate early drafts that can later be refined and improved.

This makes it possible for individuals to build useful content resources much faster than before.

Why This Works Now

People search the internet for answers every day.

They look for explanations, step-by-step guides, product comparisons, and solutions to specific problems. Search engines direct users toward websites that provide clear and helpful information.

Businesses recognize the value of this traffic. As a result, many websites earn money through:

- advertising
- affiliate links
- digital products
- sponsorships
- memberships or subscriptions

AI tools make it easier to produce organized content and explore many potential article topics quickly.

However, successful niche websites still require human judgment.

Someone must decide which topics are worth covering, refine the writing, and ensure the information is accurate and genuinely helpful.

AI can accelerate production, but long-term success still depends on providing **useful, trustworthy content** for readers.

Who This Is Best For

This starting point works well for people who:

- enjoy learning about specific topics
- like organizing information into helpful explanations
- are patient with projects that grow gradually
- enjoy writing, editing, or teaching ideas

It can also be a good fit for people who already have knowledge or interest in a particular field.

For example, someone interested in gardening might build a site focused on beginner gardening advice. Someone interested in fitness might create content about home workouts.

The more clearly a website focuses on a specific niche, the easier it is for readers to understand what it offers.

What You Need

Building a niche content website requires a few basic elements.

You need:

- a website platform or blog system
- an AI writing or research tool
- a topic or niche audience to focus on
- time to create and improve content

Many websites begin with a small number of articles and grow gradually over time.

AI can help accelerate early drafting and idea generation, but careful editing and clear structure are still important.

Readers return to websites that feel **reliable, helpful, and easy to understand**.

How to Start in 24 Hours

You can begin exploring this opportunity with a simple process.

Step 1: Choose a niche topic

Pick a subject that people often search for online.

Examples include:

- beginner fitness routines
- travel planning tips
- budgeting strategies
- pet care advice

Step 2: Brainstorm article ideas

Ask AI to suggest questions people commonly ask about your topic.

Step 3: Choose three to five article topics

Focus on practical questions people might search for.

Example:

"How to start a vegetable garden in a small space."

Step 4: Use AI to generate outlines

Create structured outlines for each article.

Step 5: Write and refine the articles

Use AI to assist with drafting, but review the writing carefully and edit it so it reads clearly and accurately.

Even a small website with a handful of helpful articles can begin attracting readers.

How to Make Your First $100

Income from niche websites often grows gradually.

One of the most common early monetization methods is **affiliate links**, where you recommend useful products and receive a small commission if someone purchases through your link.

For example:

A gardening website might recommend tools or seeds.

A fitness site might recommend workout equipment or training programs.

If a website receives steady visitors and a few readers make purchases through affiliate links, it can eventually produce its first $100.

Another option is displaying advertising through website ad networks once traffic grows.

The key is consistency. Websites often grow slowly at first, but valuable content can attract readers for months or even years.

How to Grow It

As a niche website expands, several growth opportunities may appear.
You might:

- publish more articles answering related questions
- create downloadable guides or resources
- build an email newsletter for readers
- review products related to your topic
- create digital products or courses

Over time, a niche website can become a trusted resource within a particular topic area.
Some creators eventually build entire businesses around their websites by combining content, digital products, and partnerships.

Watch-Outs
One challenge with niche websites is patience.
It often takes time for search engines and readers to discover new content. Many websites grow gradually rather than producing immediate income.
Another important consideration is quality.
Publishing large amounts of AI-generated content without careful editing can damage credibility and make the website less useful for readers.
Successful websites focus on **clarity, accuracy, and usefulness**, not simply volume.
AI should assist the process, but human judgment remains essential.

Try This Next
Ask your AI tool:
"What are ten common questions people search for about [your chosen topic]?"
Replace the bracket with a topic that interests you.

Choose one of the questions and outline a short article that answers it clearly.
This exercise will help you practice identifying useful content ideas.

Reflection Question

Think about topics you enjoy learning about or discussing with others.
Could you imagine building a website that answers common questions about that topic?
Sometimes a valuable online resource begins with a single helpful article.

This is the **twelfth of the 33 starting points.**
The next chapter explores another opportunity created by AI: **developing niche newsletters and information subscriptions.**

Starting Point #13
AI-Assisted Niche Newsletters

Difficulty: Beginner to Intermediate
Startup Cost: Low
Time to First Income: 1–3 months
Income Type: Subscription-based or Sponsorship-based

What It Is

Another opportunity created by AI is building **niche newsletters** that share useful information with a specific audience.

A newsletter is a regularly delivered email publication that provides insights, updates, or curated information about a particular topic. Many newsletters focus on helping readers stay informed, learn something new, or discover useful tools and ideas.

Examples of newsletter topics might include:

- personal finance tips
- technology trends
- fitness and wellness strategies
- AI tools and productivity ideas
- industry news for a specific profession

In the past, producing a consistent newsletter required significant time. Writers had to research topics, organize ideas, and draft each issue from scratch.

AI tools can now assist with many parts of that process. They can help gather ideas, summarize articles, outline content, and generate drafts that the creator can refine and personalize.

This makes it easier for individuals to publish newsletters regularly and build an audience over time.

Why This Works Now

Email newsletters have become an important way for creators and businesses to connect directly with their audiences.

Unlike social media platforms, where algorithms determine what people see, newsletters arrive directly in a reader's inbox. This gives creators a more reliable way to communicate with their audience.

Many successful newsletters earn money through:

- paid subscriptions
- sponsorships or advertising
- affiliate recommendations
- promoting products or services

AI tools make it easier to gather information, organize insights, and draft content efficiently.

However, the real value of a newsletter still comes from the creator's perspective. Readers subscribe because they trust the writer's ability to select useful information and explain it clearly.

AI can support that process, but human judgment and voice remain essential.

Who This Is Best For

This starting point works well for people who:

- enjoy staying informed about a specific topic
- like sharing useful ideas or resources with others
- are comfortable writing short explanations or summaries
- are interested in building an audience over time

You do not need to be a professional journalist or expert to begin.

Many successful newsletters are written by people who are simply curious learners. They research topics carefully, share useful insights, and explain ideas in a clear and approachable way.

If you enjoy discovering helpful information and sharing it with others, a newsletter can become a valuable platform.

What You Need

Starting a niche newsletter requires only a few basic tools. You need:

- an email newsletter platform
- an AI tool for research and drafting support
- a clear topic or audience focus
- a consistent publishing schedule

Some creators publish weekly newsletters, while others publish twice per month.

Consistency matters more than frequency. Readers appreciate knowing when to expect new issues.

Over time, a newsletter often becomes more valuable as the audience grows.

How to Start in 24 Hours

You can begin exploring this opportunity with a simple process.

Step 1: Choose a niche topic

Pick a subject you enjoy learning about or following regularly.

Examples include:

- productivity tools
- healthy habits
- travel deals
- small business advice
- emerging technology

Step 2: Identify your audience

Ask yourself who might benefit from the information you plan to share.

Step 3: Ask AI for content ideas
Use AI to generate potential newsletter topics, common reader questions, or summaries of recent developments in your field.
Step 4: Draft your first issue
Create a simple newsletter that includes:

- one main idea or insight
- a few helpful links or resources
- a short personal explanation or takeaway

Step 5: Share it with a small audience
Send the newsletter to friends, colleagues, or early subscribers.
The goal is simply to begin publishing and learning what readers find useful.

How to Make Your First $100
Many newsletters start by building a small audience before generating income.
Once readers begin subscribing and engaging with your content, several monetization options become possible.
For example:
A newsletter with a few hundred engaged readers may attract small sponsorship opportunities.
You might also recommend products or services related to your topic using affiliate links.
Another option is offering **a paid version of the newsletter** that includes deeper insights or exclusive content.
Even a small number of paid subscribers can quickly reach your first $100.
For example:
10 subscribers paying $10 per month would generate $100 in revenue.

How to Grow It

As your newsletter audience grows, additional opportunities may emerge.
You might:

- introduce premium content for paying subscribers
- partner with companies for sponsorships
- create digital products related to your topic
- build a community around your newsletter
- host workshops, webinars, or events

Some newsletters eventually grow into full businesses that include podcasts, courses, consulting services, or media brands.
The key is building **trust and consistency** with your readers.

Watch-Outs

One common challenge with newsletters is consistency.
Publishing regularly requires commitment, and audiences may lose interest if updates become irregular.
Another important consideration is originality.
AI can assist with summarizing information and generating ideas, but your newsletter should still reflect your perspective and voice.
Readers subscribe because they value the human behind the content.
AI should support your work, not replace your point of view.

Try This Next

Ask your AI tool:
"What are five useful topics for a weekly newsletter about [your chosen niche]?"
Choose one topic and outline a short newsletter issue that explains the idea clearly and provides useful insights.
This exercise will help you practice structuring a newsletter.

Reflection Question
Think about the topics you enjoy learning about each week. Could you imagine sharing insights about that subject with others through a short email publication?
Sometimes a simple newsletter can grow into a trusted resource for a specific audience.

This is the **thirteenth of the 33 starting points.**
The next chapter explores another opportunity created by AI: **building prompt libraries and AI toolkits that can be sold as digital products.**

Starting Point #14
Selling AI Prompt Libraries

Difficulty: Beginner to Intermediate
Startup Cost: Low
Time to First Income: 1–4 weeks
Income Type: Product-based

What It Is

Another opportunity created by AI is building and selling **prompt libraries**.

A prompt library is a collection of carefully designed instructions that help people use AI tools more effectively. These prompts guide AI systems to produce useful outputs such as written content, marketing ideas, research summaries, images, or structured plans.

While many people are curious about AI tools, they often struggle with how to use them well. Writing effective prompts usually takes practice, experimentation, and refinement.

That creates an opportunity for people who are willing to test, improve, and organize prompts into useful collections.

In this model, the creator develops a set of prompts designed for a specific purpose or audience. Those prompts are then packaged into a digital product that others can purchase and use.

The value comes from helping users save time, reduce frustration, and get better results from the AI tools they are already using.

Why This Works Now

AI tools are becoming widely available, but many users are still learning how to interact with them effectively.

A well-written prompt can dramatically improve the quality of an AI-generated result. The difference between a vague instruction and a carefully structured prompt can be the difference between an unusable output and something genuinely helpful.

Because of this, many people are interested in prompts that already work well.

Prompt libraries simplify the process. Instead of experimenting from scratch every time, users can start with tested prompts designed for specific tasks.

Examples might include prompts for:

- writing marketing content
- generating business ideas
- creating lesson plans
- summarizing research
- drafting social media posts

AI tools will continue to evolve, but the ability to ask better questions and structure more effective prompts will remain valuable.

Who This Is Best For

This starting point works well for people who:

- enjoy experimenting with AI tools
- like organizing ideas into useful systems
- enjoy teaching others how to work more effectively
- are interested in creating digital products

You do not need to be a technical expert to build a prompt library.

The most valuable skill is learning how to refine prompts through experimentation and observing which instructions consistently produce useful results.

If you enjoy exploring how AI responds to different phrasing and formats, this opportunity can be both practical and creative.

What You Need

The basic setup for creating a prompt library is simple.
You need:

- an AI tool for testing prompts
- a document or design tool to organize the prompts
- a platform where the product can be sold or shared
- a specific audience or use case to focus on

Most prompt libraries are packaged as downloadable documents, worksheets, or simple digital guides.
The key is organizing the prompts clearly so users understand how and when to use them.

How to Start in 24 Hours

You can begin exploring this opportunity with a simple experiment.

Step 1: Choose a niche

Think about a group of people who might benefit from AI prompts.
Examples include:

- marketers
- teachers
- small business owners
- writers
- students

Step 2: Identify common tasks

Consider the tasks these users perform regularly.
For example:

- generating social media content
- brainstorming business ideas
- writing outlines or reports

Step 3: Develop several prompts
Use AI to help you test and refine prompts that consistently produce useful results.
Step 4: Organize the prompts
Group them into categories and write brief instructions explaining how to use them.
Step 5: Package the collection
Create a simple digital guide that includes the prompts and short explanations.
Even a small prompt collection can become a useful resource if it solves a specific problem clearly.

How to Make Your First $100

Prompt libraries are typically sold as digital products.
For example:
A prompt pack priced at $10 would need only 10 sales to reach $100.
A more specialized prompt collection priced at $20 would need only five sales.
These products can be sold through digital marketplaces, personal websites, or creator platforms.
The goal at the beginning is not to create a massive library. It is to build a small collection that solves a specific problem for a clearly defined audience.

How to Grow It

If a prompt library proves useful, it can expand in several directions.
You might:

- create additional prompt collections for different audiences
- bundle multiple prompt libraries together
- create tutorials showing how to use the prompts

- build a larger toolkit around AI productivity

Some creators eventually build full educational products or communities around teaching people how to use AI tools more effectively.

Over time, a well-designed prompt system can become part of a larger library of digital resources.

Watch-Outs

One common mistake is creating prompts that are too vague or generic.

Prompts become valuable when they are specific and clearly designed for a particular task, audience, or result.

Another challenge is organization.

A list of random prompts can feel confusing or incomplete.

The most useful prompt libraries include clear explanations and examples showing how each prompt should be used.

Finally, remember that prompt libraries may need to evolve over time.

As AI tools improve, updating and refining your prompt collections can help keep them useful and relevant.

Try This Next

Ask your AI tool:

"Create five prompts that would help a small business owner generate marketing ideas."

Test the prompts and refine them until they produce helpful results.

This simple exercise will help you begin building your own prompt collection.

Reflection Question

Think about the ways you currently use AI.

Are there prompts that consistently produce helpful results for you?

Organizing those prompts into a clear system may turn them into a useful resource for others.

This is the **fourteenth of the 33 starting points.**
The next chapter explores another opportunity created by AI: **developing simple automation workflows that help individuals or businesses save time.**

Starting Point #15

Creating Simple AI Automation Workflows

Difficulty: Intermediate
Startup Cost: Low to Medium
Time to First Income: 2–4 weeks
Income Type: Service-based or Product-based

What It Is

Another growing opportunity in the AI economy is helping individuals and businesses **automate repetitive tasks** using simple AI-powered workflows.

Many people spend a significant amount of time performing tasks that follow the same basic pattern every day. These tasks might include organizing information, responding to messages, summarizing documents, collecting data, or generating routine content.

AI tools can now assist with many of these tasks.

By connecting AI systems with other digital tools—such as email platforms, spreadsheets, document systems, or customer communication tools—it becomes possible to create simple workflows that handle part of the work automatically.

In this model, the opportunity comes from **designing helpful systems** that save people time.

The person building the workflow identifies a repetitive task, connects the right tools, and creates a process that reduces manual effort.

For busy businesses and professionals, saving time can be extremely valuable.

Why This Works Now

Automation has existed for many years, but it often required technical programming skills to build.

Today, many tools allow people to create automated workflows without writing complex code. These systems connect apps and services so they can exchange information automatically.

AI adds another layer of value.

Instead of simply moving information from one place to another, AI can now help interpret, summarize, generate, or categorize information as it moves through the workflow.

For example, an automated system might:

- summarize incoming emails
- generate draft responses to customer inquiries
- organize notes from meeting transcripts
- categorize documents or messages
- generate simple reports based on collected information

These kinds of systems can significantly reduce the amount of routine work people must do manually.

Because many businesses are still learning how to apply these tools, there is growing demand for people who can design simple automation solutions.

Who This Is Best For

This starting point works well for people who:

- enjoy solving practical problems
- like improving systems and processes
- are curious about how digital tools connect with each other
- enjoy experimenting with technology and workflows

You do not need to be a professional programmer to begin exploring automation.

Many automation tools are designed to be visual and user-friendly, allowing people to build workflows by connecting steps together.
If you enjoy finding ways to simplify repetitive tasks, this type of work can be both satisfying and valuable.

What You Need
The setup for building simple automation workflows typically includes:

- one or more AI tools
- a workflow automation platform
- familiarity with common business tools such as email, documents, or spreadsheets
- time to experiment and test different processes

You may also want to document your workflows so clients or users understand how the system works.
Clear explanations help people trust and use the systems you create.

How to Start in 24 Hours
You can begin exploring automation opportunities by identifying repetitive tasks in everyday work.
Step 1: Identify a repetitive task
Look for activities that follow the same pattern repeatedly.
Examples might include:

- sorting emails
- organizing notes
- summarizing meeting transcripts
- generating routine reports

Step 2: Map the process
Write down each step in the task so you understand how it currently works.

Step 3: Ask AI how the task could be automated
Use AI to suggest ways to simplify or automate the process using available tools.
Step 4: Build a simple workflow
Experiment with connecting the tools involved in the process.
Step 5: Test and refine
Run the workflow several times to make sure it works consistently.
Even a small improvement that saves a few minutes per task can create meaningful value over time.

How to Make Your First $100

One way to generate early income from automation is by helping a small business streamline a specific process.
For example:
A local business might pay $50–$100 to set up a system that automatically organizes incoming customer inquiries.
Another example could be creating a workflow that summarizes meeting notes and sends a short report to a team.
Even small automation projects can create noticeable time savings, which makes them attractive to clients.
Completing just one or two simple workflow projects could easily produce your first $100.

How to Grow It

If you enjoy building automation workflows, this opportunity can expand in several directions.
You might:

- specialize in automation for a specific industry
- build workflow templates that can be reused for multiple clients
- offer ongoing system optimization or consulting

- create tutorials or digital products that teach others how to build similar workflows

Some automation specialists eventually develop larger productivity systems for businesses.

Over time, your value increases as you gain more experience identifying opportunities to simplify repetitive processes.

Watch-Outs

One common mistake in automation projects is trying to automate tasks that are not clearly defined.

A workflow works best when the underlying process is simple, consistent, and easy to understand.

Another challenge is overcomplicating the system.

The most effective automation solutions are often the simplest ones—systems that solve one clear problem reliably.

Finally, remember that automation still requires human oversight.

AI tools can assist with processing information, but people should still review important outputs to ensure accuracy.

Try This Next

Ask your AI tool:

"What are three repetitive tasks that small businesses could automate using AI tools?"

Choose one of the ideas and map out the steps involved.

This exercise will help you begin thinking like a workflow designer.

Reflection Question

Think about the tasks you perform regularly that feel repetitive or time-consuming.

If those tasks could be simplified or automated, how much time might you save?
Sometimes the best automation ideas begin by improving the work you already do.

This is the **fifteenth of the 33 starting points.**
The next chapter explores another opportunity created by AI: **using AI to assist with data organization and analysis for businesses and professionals.**

Starting Point #16
AI-Assisted Data Organization and Analysis

Difficulty: Intermediate
Startup Cost: Low
Time to First Income: 2–4 weeks
Income Type: Service-based

What It Is

Another opportunity created by AI is helping individuals and businesses **organize and analyze data more effectively**. Many organizations collect large amounts of information. This might include customer feedback, survey responses, sales records, research notes, or operational reports. While this data can be valuable, it is often scattered across documents, spreadsheets, or databases that are difficult to interpret.

AI tools can help process and organize this information much more quickly.

They can summarize documents, identify patterns in text, categorize information, and highlight key insights. When combined with careful human review, these tools can transform large amounts of raw data into clear summaries and useful reports.

In this model, the opportunity comes from helping others make sense of information that would otherwise take significant time to analyze manually.

Why This Works Now

Modern businesses generate more data than ever before. Customer surveys, online reviews, analytics reports, meeting notes, and internal documents all produce information that can help organizations make better decisions. However, many teams struggle to review and interpret this information efficiently.

AI tools make it easier to analyze large amounts of text or structured data quickly.

For example, AI can help:

- summarize customer feedback
- identify common themes in survey responses
- organize research notes into structured categories
- extract key insights from reports or transcripts
- generate clear summaries of complex information

These capabilities can significantly reduce the time required to review and interpret data.

Because many organizations lack the time or expertise to perform this type of analysis themselves, there is growing demand for people who can assist with organizing and interpreting information.

Who This Is Best For

This starting point works well for people who:

- enjoy working with information and patterns
- like organizing complex material into clear summaries
- are comfortable reviewing data carefully
- enjoy analytical thinking

It can also be a strong fit for people with experience in research, consulting, marketing, education, or project management.

You do not need to be a data scientist to begin. Many useful projects involve organizing qualitative information such as written feedback, documents, or transcripts.

The key skill is turning scattered information into insights that people can understand and use.

What You Need

The basic setup for AI-assisted data analysis includes:

- an AI tool capable of summarizing and analyzing information
- access to the data or documents you want to analyze
- a spreadsheet, document editor, or reporting format
- the ability to review results carefully for accuracy

In many cases, the final deliverable is a short report that highlights key patterns, summaries, or recommendations. Clear presentation is just as important as the analysis itself.

How to Start in 24 Hours

You can begin exploring this opportunity by practicing with sample data.

Step 1: Find a data example

This could be survey responses, customer reviews, meeting notes, or research documents.

Step 2: Ask AI to summarize the information

Use AI to identify themes, trends, or recurring ideas within the data.

Step 3: Organize the results

Group similar insights together and create categories that help explain the information.

Step 4: Create a short summary report

Write a clear explanation of the key findings.

Step 5: Refine the report

Make sure the insights are accurate and easy to understand.
This process transforms raw information into something that decision-makers can quickly understand and use.

How to Make Your First $100

One way to begin earning from this skill is by offering small analysis projects.

For example:

A business might pay $50–$100 to analyze customer feedback and produce a short summary report.

Another example might involve reviewing survey results and highlighting the most common responses.

These projects can often be completed relatively quickly using AI-assisted analysis.

Completing one or two small projects can easily help you reach your first $100.

How to Grow It

As you gain experience with data analysis, this opportunity can expand in several directions.

You might:

- specialize in analyzing feedback or survey results
- provide research summaries for writers or consultants
- create reports for marketing or product teams
- develop dashboards or recurring reports for businesses

Some professionals eventually turn this skill into a larger consulting service focused on business insights or decision support.

Over time, the ability to interpret information clearly can become extremely valuable.

Watch-Outs

One important challenge in data analysis is accuracy.

AI can help identify patterns, but the results should always be reviewed carefully. Misinterpreting information can lead to incorrect conclusions.
Another challenge is context.
Data rarely tells the full story on its own. Understanding the purpose of the data and the questions being asked is essential for meaningful analysis.
Finally, avoid overwhelming clients with too much raw information.
The value of your work comes from presenting **clear insights**, not just large amounts of data.

Try This Next
Ask your AI tool:
"Analyze these customer reviews and identify the five most common themes mentioned by customers."
Then review the results and organize them into a short summary.
This exercise will help you practice turning raw information into useful insights.

Reflection Question
Think about the types of information people regularly collect in their work.
Customer feedback, surveys, reports, and research often contain valuable insights that can be difficult to interpret quickly.
Helping people understand their own data may be one of the most useful services you can offer.

This is the **sixteenth of the 33 starting points.**
The next chapter explores another opportunity created by AI:

using AI to support online education and learning resources.

Starting Point #17

Using AI to Create Online Learning Resources

Difficulty: Beginner to Intermediate
Startup Cost: Low
Time to First Income: 2–6 weeks
Income Type: Product-based or Service-based

What It Is

Another opportunity created by AI is using it to **develop educational content and learning resources**.

Online learning has expanded rapidly in recent years. Students, professionals, and lifelong learners regularly search for explanations, tutorials, guides, and structured materials to help them understand new topics.

These resources can take many forms, including:

- study guides
- tutorials
- lesson plans
- practice exercises
- short courses
- instructional videos
- learning worksheets

Traditionally, creating these materials required significant time and planning. Educators had to design outlines, develop explanations, create examples, and structure lessons carefully.

AI tools can now assist with many parts of that process. They can help generate lesson outlines, summarize complex topics, draft explanations, and create practice questions that educators can refine and organize.

In this model, AI helps accelerate content creation while the human creator ensures the material is clear, accurate, and genuinely helpful.

Why This Works Now

Education has increasingly moved online.

People are constantly learning new skills for work, school, or personal development. Many learners prefer short, focused resources that help them understand specific topics quickly.

At the same time, teachers, tutors, and subject experts often do not have enough time to produce large amounts of educational material.

AI tools make it easier to create structured learning content efficiently.

For example, AI can help:

- outline lesson plans
- draft explanations of complex ideas
- generate quiz questions or practice exercises
- summarize textbooks or articles
- create step-by-step tutorials

These capabilities allow individuals to develop educational resources more quickly than before.

Because learning materials are always in demand, well-designed resources can become valuable products or services.

Who This Is Best For

This starting point works well for people who:

- enjoy explaining ideas clearly
- have knowledge of or interest in a particular subject
- enjoy teaching or helping others learn
- like organizing information into structured formats

It can be especially useful for teachers, tutors, professionals, or subject enthusiasts who already have experience in a specific field.

However, you do not need to be a formal educator to begin. Many successful learning resources focus on practical topics such as productivity tools, career skills, hobbies, or beginner-level knowledge.

The key is presenting information in a way that helps others understand it more easily.

What You Need

The basic setup for creating online learning resources includes:

- an AI tool for outlining and drafting content
- a document or design platform for organizing the material
- a platform where the resource can be shared or sold
- knowledge of the topic you want to teach

Educational materials can be simple at first. Many creators begin with downloadable guides, short tutorials, or structured worksheets.

Over time, these resources can grow into larger learning products.

How to Start in 24 Hours

You can begin exploring this opportunity by developing a simple learning resource.

Step 1: Choose a topic

Select a subject you understand or enjoy learning about. Examples might include:

- beginner financial planning
- productivity tools
- study strategies
- basic programming concepts
- hobby skills such as photography or cooking

Step 2: Ask AI to outline a lesson

Use AI to generate a structured outline that explains the topic step by step.

Step 3: Expand the explanations

Write or refine the explanations so they are clear and easy to understand.

Step 4: Add examples or exercises

Include simple practice questions, examples, or short activities.

Step 5: Organize the material

Package the content into a guide, worksheet, or tutorial that someone else could follow.

Even a short resource can be valuable if it explains a topic clearly.

How to Make Your First $100

Educational resources can generate income in several ways.

For example:

A downloadable study guide priced at $10 would require only 10 sales to reach $100.

A small tutorial or mini-course priced at $25 would need four sales.

Another option is offering tutoring sessions or consulting based on the material you create.

In many cases, the first step is building a resource that demonstrates your ability to explain a topic effectively.

How to Grow It

If your educational materials prove useful, this opportunity can expand in several directions.

You might:

- create additional guides or tutorials on related topics
- develop a full online course
- offer workshops or group learning sessions

- build a library of educational resources
- create a learning community around your topic

Some creators eventually turn educational content into full businesses that include courses, memberships, coaching, or certification programs.

The key is building resources that genuinely help people learn and apply new knowledge.

Watch-Outs

One challenge when creating educational content is accuracy.

AI can help generate explanations, but the information should always be reviewed carefully to ensure it is correct and up to date.

Another common mistake is trying to teach too much at once.

Effective learning materials often focus on one specific topic and explain it clearly rather than covering many ideas too quickly.

Finally, remember that good teaching requires empathy. Understanding the learner's perspective and explaining concepts simply can make a resource far more valuable.

Try This Next

Ask your AI tool:

"Create an outline for a beginner lesson explaining [your chosen topic]."

Then expand the outline into a short guide or tutorial.

This exercise will help you practice structuring educational content.

Reflection Question

Think about the topics you understand well enough to explain to someone else.
If you could help a beginner learn that topic more easily, what would the first lesson look like?
Sometimes a valuable educational resource begins with one clear explanation.

This is the **seventeenth of the 33 starting points.**
The next chapter explores another opportunity created by AI: **helping businesses improve marketing and advertising through AI-assisted analysis and content creation.**

Starting Point #18
AI-Assisted Marketing and Advertising

Difficulty: Beginner to Intermediate
Startup Cost: Low
Time to First Income: 1–3 weeks
Income Type: Service-based or Product-based

What It Is

Another opportunity created by AI is helping businesses improve their **marketing and advertising efforts**.
Marketing is essential for almost every business. Companies need to communicate with customers, promote their products or services, and attract attention in competitive markets. This often requires creating content, generating ideas, analyzing performance, and adjusting strategies.
AI tools can assist with many of these tasks.
They can help generate marketing ideas, draft advertising copy, suggest campaign strategies, analyze customer feedback, and produce content for social media or email campaigns.
In this model, AI acts as a powerful brainstorming and production tool, while the human marketer provides strategy, judgment, and creative direction.
The opportunity comes from helping businesses use AI to make their marketing more efficient and more effective.

Why This Works Now

Marketing requires a constant flow of new ideas and content.
Businesses regularly need:

- social media posts
- advertising headlines
- promotional emails
- product descriptions

- marketing strategies
- audience insights

Creating this material can take significant time.
AI tools can accelerate the early stages of the process. They can generate drafts, suggest variations, and help organize campaign ideas quickly.
For example, AI can help marketers:

- generate multiple advertising headlines
- brainstorm campaign ideas
- draft social media posts
- analyze customer reviews or feedback
- create outlines for marketing plans

This allows marketers and business owners to focus more on strategy and refinement instead of starting from a blank page every time.
Because many small businesses do not have dedicated marketing teams, there is growing demand for people who can help them improve their marketing processes.

Who This Is Best For
This starting point works well for people who:

- enjoy creative thinking and communication
- are interested in marketing or advertising
- like experimenting with ideas and messaging
- enjoy analyzing customer behavior or feedback

It can be a particularly good fit for freelancers, consultants, content creators, or anyone interested in business strategy.
You do not need to be an expert marketer to begin. Many successful marketing services focus on simple improvements such as better messaging, more consistent content, or clearer communication with customers.
The key is helping businesses communicate their value more effectively.

What You Need

The setup for AI-assisted marketing work is relatively simple. You need:

- one or more AI tools for brainstorming and drafting
- a basic understanding of marketing goals and audiences
- the ability to review and refine AI-generated content
- a way to communicate with clients or businesses

You may also benefit from learning basic marketing principles such as audience targeting, clear messaging, and persuasive writing.

AI can help generate ideas, but human judgment is still necessary to ensure the marketing is effective and appropriate for the audience.

How to Start in 24 Hours

You can begin exploring this opportunity by creating a simple marketing example.

Step 1: Choose a type of business

Examples might include:

- a local restaurant
- a fitness coach
- a landscaping company
- a small online store

Step 2: Ask AI to generate marketing ideas

Request suggestions for promotions, campaigns, or messaging strategies.

Step 3: Create sample content

Use AI to draft social media posts, advertising headlines, or promotional emails.

Step 4: Refine the content
Edit the results so they sound natural, clear, and appropriate for the business.
Step 5: Present the example
Show the marketing ideas to a business owner or include them in a simple portfolio.
This small exercise helps demonstrate how AI can support practical marketing work.

How to Make Your First $100

One way to begin earning is by offering simple marketing services to small businesses.
For example:
You might offer a **social media content package** for $50 that includes several posts and captions.
Completing two small projects could take you to your first $100.
Another option is helping a business generate advertising ideas or short promotional campaigns.
Because many small businesses struggle with consistent marketing, even simple improvements can be valuable.

How to Grow It

If you enjoy marketing work, this opportunity can grow in several directions.
You might:

- manage social media accounts for businesses
- develop marketing strategies or campaign plans
- analyze customer feedback and messaging
- create advertising content or email campaigns
- specialize in marketing for a specific industry

Some people eventually build marketing agencies or consulting businesses that combine AI tools with traditional marketing expertise.
Over time, your value increases as you learn how messaging, creativity, and strategy work together.

Watch-Outs

One common mistake is relying too heavily on AI-generated content without refining it.
Marketing messages need to feel authentic and aligned with the brand's voice. Raw AI output often requires editing and adjustment.
Another challenge is understanding the audience.
Marketing works best when it connects with the specific needs, interests, and motivations of customers. AI can generate ideas, but human insight is essential for choosing the best ones.
Finally, avoid producing large amounts of generic content.
Effective marketing focuses on **clear messaging and real value**, not just volume.

Try This Next

Ask your AI tool:
"Generate five marketing campaign ideas for a local [type of business]."
Then choose one idea and expand it into a short campaign plan.
This exercise will help you practice thinking like a marketer.

Reflection Question

Think about the businesses you interact with regularly.
How could their marketing messages be clearer, more engaging, or more consistent?

Helping businesses communicate their value effectively may become one of the most useful ways to apply AI tools.

This is the **eighteenth of the 33 starting points**.
The next chapter explores another opportunity created by AI: **using AI to assist with research and information gathering for professionals and businesses.**

Starting Point #19
AI-Assisted Research Services

Difficulty: Beginner to Intermediate
Startup Cost: Low
Time to First Income: 1–3 weeks
Income Type: Service-based

What It Is

Another opportunity created by AI is providing **research and information-gathering services** for individuals and businesses.

Research is a critical part of many kinds of work. Businesses need to understand markets, competitors, customer behavior, and industry trends. Writers, consultants, students, and professionals often need to gather and organize information before making decisions or producing reports.

Traditionally, research could take many hours or even days. It often involved searching through articles, reports, and documents to locate relevant insights.

AI tools can now assist with many parts of that process. They can help summarize articles, identify patterns across multiple sources, organize information into categories, and generate structured reports that make complex topics easier to understand.

In this model, AI accelerates the research process while the human researcher reviews the information, verifies accuracy, and organizes the final insights.

The value comes from saving clients time and helping them access useful information more quickly.

Why This Works Now

The amount of information available online continues to grow rapidly.

Businesses and professionals are surrounded by articles, reports, reviews, and data sources. While this information can be valuable, it can also be overwhelming to sort through. AI tools can help process large amounts of information quickly.

For example, AI can assist with:

- summarizing articles or research papers
- comparing multiple sources of information
- identifying trends across reports or reviews
- organizing research into structured notes
- generating concise summaries of complex topics

These capabilities allow researchers to move through the early stages of information gathering much faster.

Because many professionals do not have the time to perform detailed research themselves, there is growing demand for people who can help gather and organize insights efficiently.

Who This Is Best For

This starting point works well for people who:

- enjoy learning about new topics
- like gathering and organizing information
- are curious and detail-oriented
- enjoy explaining complex ideas clearly

It can be particularly useful for people with backgrounds in writing, consulting, education, journalism, or business analysis.

However, you do not need formal research training to begin. Many research tasks involve organizing publicly available information into clear summaries that help others make decisions.

The key skill is identifying useful information and presenting it in a way that saves the client time.

What You Need

The setup for AI-assisted research work is relatively simple. You need:

- an AI tool capable of summarizing and analyzing information
- access to reliable online sources
- a document or report format for presenting findings
- the ability to review and verify information carefully

Because AI can sometimes produce incomplete or inaccurate summaries, careful human review is essential. Clients rely on the researcher to ensure the final report is accurate, useful, and easy to understand.

How to Start in 24 Hours

You can begin exploring this opportunity by practicing with a small research project.

Step 1: Choose a topic

Select a subject that businesses or professionals might want to understand better.

Examples might include:

- emerging trends in a particular industry
- customer preferences for a type of product
- competitor offerings in a local market
- new tools or technologies in a field

Step 2: Ask AI to gather initial insights

Use AI to summarize articles or generate an overview of the topic.

Step 3: Collect additional sources

Identify several reliable sources that support or expand on the topic.

Step 4: Organize the findings

Group related ideas together and identify the most important insights.

Step 5: Write a short research summary

Create a concise report that explains the key points clearly.

This exercise helps you practice turning scattered information into a useful research brief.

How to Make Your First $100

Research services are often sold as small projects.

For example:

A business owner might pay $50–$100 for a short report summarizing competitors or market trends.

Another example might involve gathering information about potential suppliers, tools, or strategies related to a business decision.

Because AI speeds up the research process, many of these projects can be completed relatively quickly.

Completing one or two small research projects could easily help you reach your first $100.

How to Grow It

If you enjoy research work, this opportunity can expand in several directions.

You might:

- specialize in research for a particular industry
- provide competitive analysis for businesses
- assist writers or consultants with background research
- create research reports or briefing documents
- combine research with consulting or strategic insights

Over time, the ability to quickly gather and interpret useful information can become a highly valuable professional skill.

Many businesses rely on research to guide important decisions, which means skilled researchers are often in demand.

Watch-Outs

One important challenge in research work is **accuracy**.
AI tools can help summarize information, but the results should always be verified using reliable sources.
Another challenge is **information overload**.
Clients do not usually want large collections of raw data.
They want clear insights that help them understand the topic quickly.
Your value comes from organizing information into concise, understandable conclusions.
Finally, avoid presenting speculation as fact.
Careful verification and responsible interpretation are essential for trustworthy research.

Try This Next

Ask your AI tool:
"Summarize the key trends in the [industry or topic] over the past five years."
Then review the summary and verify the information using reliable sources.
This exercise will help you practice turning research into structured insights.

Reflection Question

Think about decisions that businesses or professionals often need to make.
What types of information would help them make those decisions more confidently?
Providing clear research and organized insights may become one of the most valuable services you can offer.

This is the **nineteenth of the 33 starting points.**
The next chapter explores another opportunity created by AI: **helping individuals and businesses improve customer support and communication using AI tools.**

Starting Point #20
AI-Assisted Customer Support and Communication

Difficulty: Beginner to Intermediate
Startup Cost: Low
Time to First Income: 1–3 weeks
Income Type: Service-based

What It Is

Another opportunity created by AI is helping businesses improve their **customer support and communication systems**.

Most businesses regularly communicate with customers through email, messaging platforms, websites, or social media. These conversations often involve answering common questions, responding to complaints, providing updates, or guiding customers through purchases.

While customer communication is essential, it can also be time-consuming.

AI tools can help businesses manage these interactions more efficiently. They can assist with drafting responses, organizing incoming messages, summarizing conversations, and helping teams respond more quickly and consistently.

In this model, the opportunity comes from helping businesses **design better communication workflows** using AI tools.

Instead of replacing human interaction, AI supports it by handling repetitive tasks and helping teams respond more efficiently.

Why This Works Now

Customer expectations for fast responses have increased.

People now expect businesses to reply quickly to messages, emails, and support requests. However, many small businesses do not have dedicated customer support teams. As a result, business owners often spend large portions of their day answering similar questions repeatedly.
AI tools can help streamline these interactions.
For example, AI can assist with:

- drafting responses to common customer questions
- summarizing long email threads or conversations
- organizing support requests into categories
- generating frequently asked questions (FAQ) content
- helping teams maintain consistent communication

These improvements can reduce the time businesses spend on routine communication while improving the overall customer experience.
Because many businesses are still learning how to apply AI tools in this area, there is growing demand for people who can help design simple and effective communication systems.

Who This Is Best For
This starting point works well for people who:

- enjoy helping others solve problems
- are comfortable communicating clearly in writing
- like organizing processes and workflows
- are interested in improving customer experiences

It can be a good fit for virtual assistants, freelancers, consultants, or anyone interested in business operations.

You do not need to be a technical expert to begin.
Many improvements in customer communication involve simple systems such as response templates, organized message workflows, or AI-assisted drafting tools.
The key is helping businesses communicate with customers more efficiently and consistently.

What You Need

The setup for AI-assisted customer communication work is relatively simple.
You need:

- an AI tool that can assist with writing and summarizing messages
- an understanding of common customer communication channels such as email or messaging apps
- the ability to organize common questions and responses
- a method for presenting or implementing improved workflows for clients

You may also benefit from studying examples of effective customer service communication.
Clear, friendly, and helpful responses are essential for building trust with customers.

How to Start in 24 Hours

You can begin exploring this opportunity by analyzing a simple customer support scenario.

Step 1: Choose a type of business

Examples might include:

- a local retail shop
- an online store
- a service provider such as a contractor or consultant

- a subscription-based business

Step 2: Identify common customer questions

Examples might include:

- order status inquiries
- appointment scheduling
- pricing questions
- product information requests

Step 3: Ask AI to draft response templates

Create several clear and helpful replies that businesses could use for these questions.

Step 4: Organize the responses

Structure the replies into categories such as FAQs or response templates.

Step 5: Present the system

Share the example with a business owner or include it in a simple portfolio to demonstrate how AI can improve communication.

This exercise helps you practice designing simple support systems.

How to Make Your First $100

Many small businesses struggle with customer communication simply because they lack clear systems.

You might offer services such as:

- creating a set of AI-assisted response templates
- organizing common questions into a FAQ system
- helping a business structure its customer communication process

A simple project helping a business organize their customer support responses could easily be worth $50–$100.

Completing one or two small projects could help you reach your first $100.

How to Grow It

If you enjoy improving communication systems, this opportunity can expand in several directions.

You might:

- help businesses design customer support workflows
- create AI-assisted response systems
- develop training materials for customer service teams
- build communication templates for specific industries
- combine customer support optimization with automation tools

Over time, improving customer communication can become a specialized consulting service.

Businesses value systems that help them respond faster while maintaining a high-quality customer experience.

Watch-Outs

One common mistake is relying too heavily on automated responses.

Customers still value human interaction, especially when dealing with complex problems or sensitive issues.

AI should support communication, not replace thoughtful human responses.

Another challenge is tone.

Customer communication must be clear, respectful, and aligned with the business's brand voice. AI-generated responses should always be reviewed and refined before use.

Finally, avoid overcomplicating the system.

The most effective communication workflows are often the simplest ones.

Try This Next

Ask your AI tool:

"Generate five professional response templates for a business responding to common customer questions."

Review the responses and refine them so they sound natural, clear, and helpful.

This exercise will help you practice designing better communication systems.

Reflection Question

Think about the businesses you interact with regularly.

How quickly and clearly do they respond to customer questions?

Helping businesses improve communication with their customers can create meaningful value while saving them time.

This is the **twentieth of the 33 starting points.**

The next chapter explores another opportunity created by AI: **helping creators and businesses produce video and multimedia content more efficiently.**

Starting Point #21
AI-Assisted Video and Multimedia Content Creation

Difficulty: Beginner to Intermediate
Startup Cost: Low to Medium
Time to First Income: 1–3 weeks
Income Type: Service-based or Product-based

What It Is

Another opportunity created by AI is helping individuals and businesses **produce video and multimedia content more efficiently**.

Video has become one of the most powerful forms of communication online. Businesses, creators, educators, and organizations regularly use video to explain ideas, promote products, share updates, and connect with audiences.

However, creating video content traditionally required specialized skills such as scripting, filming, editing, and graphic design. These steps could make video production expensive and time-consuming.

AI tools are changing that process.

Today, AI can help generate scripts, suggest story ideas, edit video clips, create subtitles, generate visual assets, and assist with voiceovers or narration.

In this model, AI accelerates production while the human creator shapes the final message and ensures the content connects with the audience.

Why This Works Now

Online platforms increasingly prioritize video content.

Short-form video platforms, streaming services, and social media channels have created enormous demand for visual content. Businesses and creators often need a steady flow of videos to stay visible and engage their audiences.

At the same time, many people want to create videos but feel overwhelmed by the technical process.
AI tools help simplify several parts of video production.
For example, AI can assist with:

- generating video script ideas
- summarizing long content into short clips
- creating subtitles and captions automatically
- suggesting editing improvements
- generating visuals or graphics

These tools allow creators to produce videos faster while maintaining quality.
Because many businesses want video content but lack the time or expertise to create it themselves, there is growing demand for people who can help manage and produce this content.

Who This Is Best For

This starting point works well for people who:

- enjoy creative storytelling
- are interested in video, media, or visual communication
- like experimenting with new digital tools
- enjoy helping others present ideas clearly

It can be a particularly good fit for content creators, freelancers, marketers, designers, or anyone interested in media production.
You do not need to be a professional filmmaker to begin.
Many successful video creators start by producing simple, helpful content that communicates ideas clearly.
The key skill is combining AI tools with good judgment about what makes a message engaging.

What You Need

The setup for AI-assisted video creation can vary depending on the type of content you want to produce.
In most cases, you need:

- an AI tool that can assist with script writing or editing
- a video editing or media platform
- basic recording equipment such as a smartphone or microphone
- a platform where the finished video can be shared

Many AI tools can now automate parts of the editing process, making it easier to produce polished videos without advanced technical skills.
Over time, experimenting with different formats will help you discover what works best.

How to Start in 24 Hours

You can begin exploring this opportunity by creating a simple video project.

Step 1: Choose a topic

Pick a subject that businesses or audiences might find useful or interesting.
Examples might include:

- a short business tip
- a product explanation
- a quick tutorial
- a short educational concept

Step 2: Ask AI to generate a script

Use AI to outline or draft a short script for the video.

Step 3: Record or assemble the video

Use a phone, camera, or screen recording tool to create the video.

Step 4: Use AI tools to assist with editing

Generate subtitles, trim clips, or add simple visuals.

Step 5: Share the finished video

Post the video online or include it in a small portfolio.
This exercise helps you practice combining AI tools with creative storytelling.

How to Make Your First $100

Many businesses want video content but do not have the time to create it.
You might offer services such as:

- creating short promotional videos for local businesses
- producing social media clips from longer content
- editing video content using AI-assisted tools
- adding subtitles or captions to existing videos

For example:
A business might pay $50 to have two short social media videos created or edited.
Completing two projects could help you reach your first $100.
As you gain experience, the value of your services can increase significantly.

How to Grow It

If you enjoy working with video, this opportunity can expand in several directions.
You might:

- specialize in social media video content
- create promotional videos for businesses
- edit video podcasts or interviews
- develop educational video courses
- produce content for creators or influencers

Some creators eventually build media agencies or production services that combine AI tools with creative storytelling.
Over time, video production skills can become highly valuable in marketing, education, and digital media.

Watch-Outs
One challenge with AI-assisted video creation is relying too heavily on automation.
AI tools can speed up editing and scripting, but strong content still requires human creativity and judgment.
Another challenge is clarity.
Videos should communicate ideas clearly and quickly.
Overly complex editing or visuals can distract from the message.
Finally, consistency matters.
Building an audience or client base often requires producing content regularly rather than focusing on a single video.

Try This Next
Ask your AI tool:
"Create a short 60-second script explaining a useful tip for [a specific audience or topic]."
Then record or assemble a simple video based on the script.
This exercise will help you practice turning ideas into visual content.

Reflection Question
Think about the videos you watch regularly online.
What makes them clear, engaging, or memorable?
Learning to combine storytelling with AI-powered production tools may open new opportunities in digital media.

This is the **twenty-first of the 33 starting points.**
The next chapter explores another opportunity created by AI: **creating AI-powered personal productivity systems and tools.**

Starting Point #22

AI Productivity Systems for Professionals

Difficulty: Beginner to Intermediate
Startup Cost: Low
Time to First Income: 1–3 weeks
Income Type: Service-based or Product-based

What It Is

Another opportunity created by AI is helping professionals build **AI-powered productivity systems** that improve how they work each day.

Many professionals spend large portions of their time managing tasks such as writing emails, organizing notes, preparing reports, summarizing information, planning projects, and tracking ideas.

While these tasks are necessary, they can also consume significant time and mental energy.

AI tools can assist with many of these activities.

They can help draft messages, summarize documents, organize meeting notes, generate outlines for projects, and help professionals structure their daily workflows more efficiently.

In this model, the opportunity comes from helping individuals **design practical systems that combine AI tools with their existing work processes**.

Instead of replacing human effort, AI becomes a productivity partner that helps people focus on higher-value work.

Why This Works Now

Modern professionals face increasing demands on their time and attention.

Emails, meetings, reports, and project management tasks can quickly overwhelm even highly organized individuals.

AI tools offer a way to reduce the time spent on routine work. For example, AI can assist with:

- summarizing meeting notes or transcripts
- drafting professional emails or reports
- organizing research or documents
- generating outlines for presentations or proposals
- helping structure project plans

These capabilities allow professionals to complete certain tasks more quickly while maintaining quality.

Because many people are still learning how to integrate AI into their daily workflows, there is growing demand for individuals who can help design simple productivity systems.

Who This Is Best For

This starting point works well for people who:

- enjoy organizing systems and workflows
- are interested in productivity and efficiency
- like experimenting with tools and processes
- enjoy helping others work more effectively

It can be particularly useful for consultants, virtual assistants, productivity coaches, freelancers, or professionals interested in improving workplace systems.

You do not need advanced technical skills to begin.

Many productivity improvements come from simple systems that combine AI tools with clear workflows.

The key skill is understanding how work gets done and identifying where AI can reduce unnecessary effort.

What You Need

The setup for creating AI productivity systems is relatively simple.

You need:

- an AI tool that can assist with writing, summarizing, and organizing information
- familiarity with common workplace tools such as documents, email, and note systems
- the ability to design simple workflows that others can follow
- a way to explain or demonstrate the system to clients

In many cases, productivity systems involve combining several small improvements into a clear process that saves time each day.

How to Start in 24 Hours

You can begin exploring this opportunity by improving a simple workflow.

Step 1: Identify a common professional task

Examples might include:

- writing daily emails
- summarizing meetings
- organizing research notes
- planning weekly work tasks

Step 2: Ask AI to assist with the task

Experiment with prompts that help structure or simplify the process.

Step 3: Create a repeatable workflow

Write down the steps that combine AI with the existing task.

Step 4: Test the system

Use the workflow yourself or ask a colleague to try it.

Step 5: Document the process

Create a short guide that explains how the system works.

This simple exercise helps you practice building productivity systems.

How to Make Your First $100

Professionals are often willing to pay for systems that save time.

You might offer services such as:

- designing a simple AI-assisted workflow for daily tasks
- creating productivity templates or guides
- helping a professional organize their AI tools and prompts

For example:

You might charge $50 to help a client design a workflow for organizing meeting notes and follow-up emails.

Helping two clients implement simple productivity systems could help you reach your first $100.

How to Grow It

If you enjoy improving productivity systems, this opportunity can expand in several directions.

You might:

- specialize in productivity systems for specific professions
- develop templates or guides that others can purchase
- offer workshops or consulting sessions on AI productivity
- build libraries of workflows for different tasks
- create courses teaching professionals how to use AI tools effectively

Over time, productivity consulting can grow into a specialized service that helps teams and organizations work more efficiently.

Watch-Outs

One common mistake is creating systems that are too complicated.

Productivity improvements should simplify work, not add additional layers of complexity.
Another challenge is relying too heavily on AI without reviewing the results.
AI tools can assist with drafting and organizing information, but professionals must still verify accuracy and ensure the output is appropriate.
Finally, remember that every person works differently.
The best productivity systems are flexible enough to adapt to individual workflows.

Try This Next

Ask your AI tool:
"What are five ways AI could help a busy professional save time during a typical workday?"
Review the suggestions and choose one idea to test in your own workflow.
This exercise will help you identify opportunities to improve productivity.

Reflection Question

Think about the tasks that take up the most time during your workday.
Which of those tasks could be simplified or accelerated with AI tools?
Sometimes small improvements in daily workflows can create significant time savings over time.

This is the **twenty-second of the 33 starting points.**
The next chapter explores another opportunity created by AI: **helping job seekers improve resumes, applications, and career preparation using AI tools.**

Starting Point #23
AI-Assisted Resume and Job Application Services

Difficulty: Beginner to Intermediate
Startup Cost: Low
Time to First Income: 1–2 weeks
Income Type: Service-based

What It Is
Another opportunity created by AI is helping job seekers improve their **resumes, applications, and job search materials**.
Searching for a job often requires preparing several documents, including resumes, cover letters, and professional profiles. These materials need to communicate a person's skills, experience, and value to potential employers clearly and convincingly.
Many job seekers struggle with this process.
They may find it difficult to describe their experience effectively, organize their accomplishments, or tailor their materials for specific roles.
AI tools can assist with many parts of this work.
They can help draft resumes, refine bullet points, generate cover letters, improve professional summaries, and tailor applications for different positions.
In this model, the opportunity comes from helping job seekers **use AI tools effectively while ensuring the final materials are accurate, clear, and professional**.
The human role remains essential for reviewing the content, understanding the individual's real experience, and presenting it in a way that feels authentic and compelling.

Why This Works Now
Job searching has become more competitive and more complex.
Many companies now use **Applicant Tracking Systems (ATS)** to scan resumes before they reach human recruiters.
This means resumes often need clear structure and relevant keywords related to the position.

At the same time, job seekers are applying to more positions than ever before.
Preparing customized applications for multiple roles can be time-consuming.
AI tools can help speed up parts of the process by assisting with:

- rewriting resume bullet points
- generating tailored cover letters
- identifying relevant keywords from job descriptions
- summarizing experience into stronger professional statements
- refining LinkedIn or professional profiles

These tools allow job seekers to create stronger materials more quickly.
Because many people are unfamiliar with how to use AI effectively during a job search, there is growing demand for people who can guide them.

Who This Is Best For
This starting point works well for people who:

- enjoy writing and editing
- like helping others present themselves professionally
- are interested in career development or coaching
- pay attention to detail and organization

It can be a good fit for freelancers, career coaches, writers, virtual assistants, or professionals with experience in hiring or recruiting.
You do not need to be a professional recruiter to begin.
Many resume improvement services focus on helping people **organize their experience clearly and communicate their value effectively**.
The key skill is translating someone's work experience into concise, professional language.

What You Need
The setup for offering AI-assisted resume services is simple.
You need:

- an AI tool capable of writing and editing text
- an understanding of basic resume structure

- the ability to review and refine AI-generated content
- a way to communicate with clients and gather their work history

You may also benefit from studying examples of strong resumes and common hiring practices.

Because each job seeker has unique experience and goals, careful editing and personalization are essential.

How to Start in 24 Hours

You can begin exploring this opportunity by practicing with a sample resume.

Step 1: Find an example resume

Use your own resume or create a simple sample profile.

Step 2: Ask AI to improve it

Request suggestions for clearer bullet points, stronger summaries, or better organization.

Step 3: Refine the results

Edit the AI-generated content to ensure it is accurate, professional, and aligned with the person's real experience.

Step 4: Tailor it to a job description

Ask AI to help adjust the resume for a specific job posting.

Step 5: Create a simple before-and-after example

This can become part of a small portfolio showing how you help improve resumes.

Practicing this process helps you learn how AI can assist with resume development.

How to Make Your First $100

Resume improvement services are already widely used.

You might offer services such as:

- reviewing and improving a resume
- writing a customized cover letter
- optimizing a LinkedIn profile
- tailoring resumes for specific job applications

For example:

You might charge $50 to review and improve a resume.

Helping two clients update their job application materials could take you to your first $100.

Many people are willing to pay for help with job applications because strong materials can significantly improve their chances of being noticed by employers.

How to Grow It

If you enjoy helping people with career materials, this opportunity can grow in several directions.

You might:

- specialize in resumes for specific industries
- offer interview preparation services
- provide LinkedIn profile optimization
- develop career coaching packages
- create guides or templates for job seekers

Some professionals eventually build full career consulting services that support clients through the entire job search process.

Over time, your experience helping people communicate their professional value can become highly valuable.

Watch-Outs

One common mistake is relying too heavily on AI-generated content without careful review.

Resumes must accurately represent a person's real experience. AI should assist with wording and organization, but it should not invent or exaggerate qualifications.

Another challenge is producing overly generic resumes. Strong resumes are usually tailored to specific roles and industries.

Finally, remember that honesty and clarity are essential. Helping job seekers present their real accomplishments clearly is far more effective than using inflated or exaggerated language.

Try This Next

Ask your AI tool:

"Rewrite these resume bullet points to make them clearer and more results-focused."

Then compare the original and improved versions.

This exercise will help you learn how AI can assist with resume editing.

Reflection Question

Think about the challenges people face when describing their professional experience.
How could clearer language or better organization improve the way employers understand someone's qualifications?
Helping people present their experience effectively can be a valuable and meaningful service.

This is the **twenty-third of the 33 starting points.**
The next chapter explores another opportunity created by AI: **helping entrepreneurs and small businesses develop ideas, plans, and strategies using AI tools.**

Starting Point #24

AI-Assisted Business Idea and Planning Support

Difficulty: Beginner to Intermediate
Startup Cost: Low
Time to First Income: 1–3 weeks
Income Type: Service-based or Product-based

What It Is

Another opportunity created by AI is helping entrepreneurs and small business owners **develop ideas, plans, and strategies for their businesses**.

Starting or growing a business often requires significant planning. Entrepreneurs must think about market demand, potential customers, pricing strategies, marketing approaches, and operational systems.

Many people have strong ideas but struggle to turn those ideas into clear plans.

AI tools can assist with this process.

They can help brainstorm business ideas, outline business plans, analyze potential markets, generate marketing strategies, and organize the steps involved in launching a new venture.

In this model, the opportunity comes from helping entrepreneurs **use AI as a planning tool while providing structure, clarity, and guidance throughout the process**.

AI accelerates brainstorming and analysis, while the human advisor helps organize the information and ensure the plan is practical.

Why This Works Now

Entrepreneurship has become more accessible than ever before.

Many people are interested in starting online businesses, freelancing, or launching small side projects. However, the planning process can still feel overwhelming.

Business planning traditionally required significant research, writing, and organization.

AI tools now allow entrepreneurs to generate structured outlines, explore different strategies, and test ideas much more quickly.

For example, AI can help with:

- brainstorming potential business ideas
- outlining a business plan
- identifying potential customer groups
- analyzing competitors
- generating marketing strategies
- creating step-by-step launch plans

These capabilities reduce the friction that often prevents people from moving forward with their ideas.

Because many aspiring entrepreneurs are unsure how to structure their thinking, there is growing demand for people who can guide them through the process.

Who This Is Best For

This starting point works well for people who:

- enjoy brainstorming ideas and solving problems
- are interested in entrepreneurship or small business development
- like organizing complex ideas into clear plans
- enjoy helping others think strategically

It can be a strong fit for freelancers, consultants, business enthusiasts, or professionals with experience in marketing, management, or entrepreneurship.

You do not need to be an experienced business executive to begin.

Many early-stage entrepreneurs simply need help organizing their ideas and identifying practical next steps.
The key skill is helping people move from **unclear ideas to structured plans**.

What You Need
The setup for offering AI-assisted business planning support is relatively simple.
You need:

- an AI tool capable of brainstorming, outlining, and analyzing information
- a basic understanding of business concepts such as customers, pricing, and marketing
- the ability to organize information clearly
- a way to communicate with clients and understand their goals

In many cases, your role involves guiding conversations and helping entrepreneurs translate their ideas into actionable steps.

How to Start in 24 Hours
You can begin exploring this opportunity by practicing with a sample business idea.
Step 1: Choose a simple business concept
For example:

- an online store
- a freelance service
- a local service business
- a digital product idea

Step 2: Ask AI to outline a business plan
Request a simple outline that includes the target customer, value proposition, and basic marketing approach.
Step 3: Expand key sections

Use AI to generate ideas for pricing, marketing channels, and customer acquisition.

Step 4: Organize the information

Create a short, structured document that summarizes the plan.

Step 5: Refine the plan

Review the ideas and remove anything unrealistic, unclear, or unnecessary.

This process helps you practice guiding someone from a rough idea to a clearer strategy.

How to Make Your First $100

Many aspiring entrepreneurs are willing to pay for help clarifying their ideas.

You might offer services such as:

- helping someone develop a simple business plan
- brainstorming and refining a business idea
- creating a step-by-step launch roadmap
- generating a marketing or growth strategy

For example:

You might charge $50 to help someone outline a basic business plan.

Helping two clients organize their ideas could help you reach your first $100.

Often, the value comes from helping people move forward with confidence rather than staying stuck in the idea stage.

How to Grow It

If you enjoy helping people think through business ideas, this opportunity can grow in several directions.

You might:

- specialize in startup idea development

- offer business planning sessions or workshops
- create templates or guides for entrepreneurs
- provide consulting for early-stage startups
- build educational content around entrepreneurship and AI tools

Over time, you may develop a reputation for helping people move from ideas to actionable plans.

Watch-Outs

One challenge in business planning is avoiding unrealistic expectations.
AI can generate many ideas, but not every suggestion will be practical or profitable.
Careful judgment is needed to identify which ideas are worth pursuing.
Another challenge is overcomplicating the planning process.
Many successful businesses begin with simple ideas that solve clear problems.
Finally, remember that a plan is only the beginning.
Execution, learning, and adaptation are essential parts of building a successful business.

Try This Next

Ask your AI tool:
"Generate three small business ideas that could be started with less than $500."
Then choose one idea and ask AI to outline a simple business plan.
This exercise will help you practice turning ideas into structured plans.

Reflection Question

Think about the business ideas you or others have discussed in the past.
How many of those ideas never moved forward because the planning process felt unclear or overwhelming?
Helping people turn ideas into actionable plans can be one of the most empowering ways to use AI tools.

This is the **twenty-fourth of the 33 starting points**.
The next chapter explores another opportunity created by AI: **creating and selling AI-generated digital products such as guides, templates, and toolkits.**

Starting Point #25

Creating and Selling AI-Generated Digital Products

Difficulty: Beginner to Intermediate
Startup Cost: Low
Time to First Income: 1–4 weeks
Income Type: Product-based

What It Is

Another opportunity created by AI is **creating and selling digital products** such as guides, templates, toolkits, and other downloadable resources.

Digital products are items that can be created once and sold repeatedly online. Unlike physical products, they do not require inventory, shipping, or manufacturing.

Examples of digital products include:

- instructional guides
- templates and worksheets
- planning tools
- checklists
- digital planners
- creative assets

AI tools can assist with many parts of the creation process. They can help generate outlines, draft written content, suggest ideas, organize information, and assist with formatting.

In this model, the creator uses AI to accelerate development while ensuring the final product is **clear, useful, and well organized**.

The opportunity comes from identifying problems people face and creating simple resources that help solve those problems.

Why This Works Now

The market for digital products has grown rapidly.
Many people prefer resources they can download instantly and use right away. This includes entrepreneurs, students, professionals, and hobbyists.
At the same time, AI tools have made it easier to produce structured content quickly.
For example, AI can help creators:

- outline guides or instructional materials
- generate checklists or worksheets
- develop templates for common tasks
- organize complex information into simple frameworks
- brainstorm ideas for new digital products

Because these tools speed up the creation process, individuals can develop useful products with far less time than was previously required.
Platforms for selling digital products are also widely available, making it easier than ever to reach potential buyers.

Who This Is Best For

This starting point works well for people who:

- enjoy organizing information into useful formats
- like creating practical tools or resources
- are interested in online business or digital products
- enjoy helping others solve problems

It can be a particularly good fit for writers, educators, entrepreneurs, designers, or anyone who enjoys creating structured resources.
You do not need to create a large or complicated product.
Many successful digital products are **simple tools that solve one specific problem**.
The key skill is identifying what people need and presenting the solution clearly.

What You Need

The setup for creating digital products is relatively simple. You need:

- an AI tool to help brainstorm and draft ideas
- a document or design platform for formatting the product
- a marketplace or website where the product can be sold
- a specific audience or problem to focus on

Digital products are often packaged as downloadable PDFs, guides, templates, or toolkits.

The value comes from the clarity and usefulness of the information, not the complexity of the product.

How to Start in 24 Hours

You can begin exploring this opportunity by creating a simple digital resource.

Step 1: Choose a problem to solve

Think about tasks people often struggle with.

Examples might include:

- organizing a weekly schedule
- planning a small business idea
- creating social media content
- tracking personal goals

Step 2: Ask AI to outline a resource

Use AI to generate an outline for a guide, checklist, or template.

Step 3: Develop the content

Expand the outline into a clear and practical resource.

Step 4: Format the product

Organize the content into a simple document or worksheet.

Step 5: Prepare it for sharing or selling

Create a downloadable version that others can use.

Even a small resource can become a useful digital product.

How to Make Your First $100

Digital products are often sold at relatively low prices.
For example:
A guide priced at $10 would require 10 sales to reach $100.
A toolkit priced at $20 would need five sales.
Because digital products can be sold repeatedly, even small sales can accumulate over time.
Many creators begin by producing one small resource and improving it based on feedback.

How to Grow It

If your digital product proves useful, there are many ways to expand.
You might:

- create additional products on related topics
- bundle several resources together
- build a library of templates or guides
- offer courses or workshops based on the product
- develop a brand around your digital tools

Over time, a collection of digital products can become a steady source of income.
Some creators eventually build entire businesses around educational resources, productivity tools, or specialized knowledge.

Watch-Outs

One common mistake is creating products that are too broad.
Digital products tend to work best when they solve **one clear problem for a specific audience**.
Another challenge is quality.

AI can help generate content quickly, but the final product must still be edited carefully to ensure it is accurate, organized, and useful.

Finally, avoid creating products without considering the audience.

Successful digital products are built around real needs rather than generic ideas.

Try This Next

Ask your AI tool:

“Generate five ideas for simple digital products that could help people solve everyday problems.”

Choose one idea and outline what the product might include.

This exercise will help you begin thinking like a digital product creator.

Reflection Question

Think about the tasks or challenges people face in your work, hobbies, or daily life.

Could a checklist, guide, or template help make those tasks easier?

Sometimes the simplest tools become the most valuable resources.

This is the **twenty-fifth of the 33 starting points**.

The next chapter explores another opportunity created by AI: **helping creators and businesses repurpose existing content into new formats using AI tools.**

Starting Point #26

Repurposing Content With AI

Difficulty: Beginner to Intermediate
Startup Cost: Low
Time to First Income: 1–2 weeks
Income Type: Service-based or Product-based

What It Is

Another opportunity created by AI is helping creators and businesses **repurpose existing content into new formats**. Many organizations produce valuable content such as blog posts, videos, podcasts, presentations, or reports. However, that content is often used once and then left behind.

Repurposing content means **transforming existing material into new formats that can reach different audiences**.

For example, a single piece of content might become:

- a series of social media posts
- a short video or clip
- an article or blog post
- a summary or newsletter
- a checklist or guide

AI tools can assist with many parts of this process.

They can summarize long content, extract key ideas, generate shorter posts, rewrite material for different audiences, and help organize information into new formats.

In this model, the opportunity comes from helping creators and businesses **extend the value of content they have already produced**.

Instead of constantly creating new material from scratch, they can multiply the impact of what already exists.

Why This Works Now

Content creation has become an essential part of marketing, education, and communication.
Businesses and creators often publish videos, podcasts, blogs, and social media posts to stay visible online.
However, producing new content consistently can require significant time and effort.
AI tools now make it easier to transform long-form content into multiple smaller formats.
For example, AI can help:

- summarize long articles into short posts
- turn video transcripts into blog articles
- extract quotes or highlights from podcasts
- convert written content into scripts for videos
- organize ideas into newsletters or guides

These capabilities allow one piece of content to become **many different pieces of content**.
Because many creators lack the time to repurpose their work, there is growing demand for people who can help manage this process.

Who This Is Best For

This starting point works well for people who:

- enjoy working with content and communication
- like organizing and summarizing information
- are interested in media, marketing, or publishing
- enjoy helping creators expand their reach

It can be particularly useful for freelancers, content creators, social media managers, or marketing assistants.
You do not need advanced technical skills to begin.
Many repurposing projects involve reviewing existing material and using AI tools to transform it into new formats.

The key skill is recognizing how **one idea can be presented in several useful ways**.

What You Need

The setup for offering content repurposing services is relatively simple.

You need:

- an AI tool capable of summarizing or rewriting content
- access to the original material, such as articles, videos, or podcasts
- a basic understanding of content formats such as social posts, newsletters, or blog summaries
- a way to organize and deliver the finished content

In many cases, the process involves taking one long piece of content and breaking it into several smaller pieces designed for different platforms.

How to Start in 24 Hours

You can begin exploring this opportunity by practicing with an existing piece of content.

Step 1: Choose a piece of long-form content

Examples might include:

- a blog article
- a podcast episode
- a YouTube video
- a presentation or report

Step 2: Ask AI to summarize the key ideas

Identify the most important insights or themes.

Step 3: Create multiple formats

Use AI to transform the material into several new formats, such as:

- short social media posts

- a newsletter summary
- a short script for a video

Step 4: Refine the results

Edit the content so it reads naturally and fits the intended audience and platform.

Step 5: Organize the repurposed content

Create a small package of content that could be published across different channels.

This exercise helps demonstrate how one piece of content can generate many new assets.

How to Make Your First $100

Many creators and businesses already produce content but struggle to use it efficiently.

You might offer services such as:

- converting long videos into short social media clips
- turning podcasts into blog posts
- creating social media posts from articles
- summarizing reports into newsletters

For example:

A creator might pay $50 for a package of social media posts generated from a single article or video.

Helping two clients repurpose existing content could take you to your first $100.

Because repurposing saves time while increasing content output, it can be very appealing to busy creators.

How to Grow It

If you enjoy working with content, this opportunity can grow in several directions.

You might:

- specialize in repurposing content for specific platforms

- manage content strategies for creators or businesses
- create content calendars and publishing systems
- develop packages that include multiple content formats
- build an agency focused on content transformation

Over time, repurposing content can become a core part of a broader marketing and communication strategy.

Watch-Outs

One common mistake is copying or repeating content without adapting it for the platform.

Different formats require different styles. Social media posts, for example, often need shorter and more direct language than articles or reports.

Another challenge is maintaining the original voice.

AI-generated transformations should still reflect the creator's tone, message, and intent.

Finally, quality matters more than quantity.

Repurposing should improve the usefulness and reach of the content rather than simply multiplying low-quality posts.

Try This Next

Ask your AI tool:

"Take this article and generate five social media posts summarizing the key ideas."

Then review the posts and refine them so they sound natural and engaging.

This exercise will help you practice turning long content into shorter formats.

Reflection Question

Think about the content you or others regularly produce.
How much of that content is used only once?
Repurposing can allow a single idea to reach many more people in different ways.

This is the **twenty-sixth of the 33 starting points**.
The next chapter explores another opportunity created by AI: **helping businesses and creators translate and localize content for global audiences.**

Starting Point #27

Translating and Localizing Content With AI

Difficulty: Beginner to Intermediate
Startup Cost: Low
Time to First Income: 1–3 weeks
Income Type: Service-based

What It Is

Another opportunity created by AI is helping businesses and creators **translate and adapt their content for audiences in different languages and regions**.

The internet has made it possible for businesses, educators, and creators to reach audiences all over the world. However, language barriers often prevent valuable content from reaching people who would benefit from it.

Translation allows content to be understood in another language. Localization goes a step further by adapting the message so it feels natural and culturally appropriate for a specific audience.

AI tools can assist with both of these tasks.

They can translate written content, suggest more natural phrasing, adjust tone, and help adapt material for different audiences.

In this model, the opportunity comes from helping organizations **expand the reach of their content** by making it accessible to people in additional languages and regions. AI speeds up the translation process, while human oversight helps ensure that the meaning and tone remain accurate.

Why This Works Now

Global audiences are easier to reach than ever before. Businesses, online educators, and content creators often publish material that could be valuable to people in many different countries. However, producing content in multiple languages traditionally required professional translators and significant time.

AI tools have made translation much faster and more accessible.

For example, AI can help with:

- translating articles or blog posts into other languages
- adapting marketing content for different regions
- translating product descriptions for international markets
- generating subtitles for videos in multiple languages
- converting newsletters or guides into additional languages

These capabilities make it possible for creators and businesses to expand their reach without rebuilding their content from scratch.

Because many organizations want to reach global audiences but lack the time or expertise to do so, there is growing demand for people who can help manage the process.

Who This Is Best For

This starting point works well for people who:

- speak more than one language
- enjoy working with written communication
- are interested in global audiences or international markets
- pay attention to language details and tone

It can be especially valuable for bilingual individuals, translators, writers, or freelancers interested in language services.

However, even people who speak only one language can assist with parts of the workflow, such as organizing content, managing translation processes, or reviewing AI-generated drafts.

The key skill is ensuring that translated material **reads naturally and accurately in the target language**.

What You Need

The setup for offering AI-assisted translation services is relatively simple.

You need:

- an AI tool capable of translating or rewriting content
- access to the original material that needs translation
- the ability to review translations for clarity and accuracy
- familiarity with the audience or region the content is intended for

For video or audio content, you may also use tools that generate transcripts or subtitles.

Many translation projects begin with written content such as articles, websites, or marketing materials.

How to Start in 24 Hours

You can begin exploring this opportunity by practicing with a simple piece of content.

Step 1: Choose a piece of content

Examples might include:

- a short blog post
- a marketing email
- a social media post
- a product description

Step 2: Ask AI to translate the content

Generate a translation into another language.
Step 3: Review the translation
Check that the meaning and tone remain accurate.
Step 4: Adjust for clarity
Refine the language so it reads naturally for the target audience.
Step 5: Compare versions
Look at the original and translated versions to ensure the message remains consistent.
This exercise helps you understand how AI can support translation while still requiring human review.

How to Make Your First $100

Many small businesses want to reach customers in additional languages but do not know where to begin.
You might offer services such as:

- translating blog posts or articles
- translating product descriptions for online stores
- creating subtitles for videos
- adapting marketing messages for new audiences

For example:
A business might pay $50 to translate a set of product descriptions or short articles.
Completing two small translation projects could help you reach your first $100.
Because businesses increasingly operate online, multilingual content is becoming more valuable.

How to Grow It

If you enjoy working with languages, this opportunity can expand in several directions.
You might:

- specialize in translating content for specific industries
- focus on translating marketing or educational materials
- provide localization services for international audiences
- manage multilingual content for websites or online platforms
- build a small translation or localization agency

Over time, your ability to help organizations communicate across language barriers can become highly valuable.

Watch-Outs

One important challenge in translation is accuracy.
AI tools can translate text quickly, but they may miss cultural nuances or subtle meanings.
Human review is essential to ensure the message remains clear and appropriate.
Another challenge is tone.
Marketing or creative content may need additional adjustment to feel natural in different languages.
Finally, avoid assuming that direct translation is always enough.
Effective localization often requires adapting the message so it resonates with the audience.

Try This Next

Ask your AI tool:
"Translate this article into [another language] and adjust it so it sounds natural for readers in that language."
Then compare the original and translated versions to ensure the message remains clear.
This exercise will help you practice reviewing and refining AI-assisted translations.

Reflection Question
Think about the content you regularly see online.
How many valuable resources exist only in one language?
Helping creators and businesses share their ideas across languages can open entirely new audiences.

This is the **twenty-seventh of the 33 starting points**.
The next chapter explores another opportunity created by AI:
helping individuals and organizations organize and manage knowledge using AI-powered knowledge bases and documentation systems.

Starting Point #27

Translating and Localizing Content With AI

Difficulty: Beginner to Intermediate
Startup Cost: Low
Time to First Income: 1–3 weeks
Income Type: Service-based

What It Is

Another opportunity created by AI is helping businesses and creators **translate and adapt their content for audiences in different languages and regions**.

The internet has made it possible for businesses, educators, and creators to reach audiences all over the world. However, language barriers often prevent valuable content from reaching people who would benefit from it.

Translation allows content to be understood in another language. Localization goes a step further by adapting the message so it feels natural and culturally appropriate for a specific audience.

AI tools can assist with both of these tasks.

They can translate written content, suggest more natural phrasing, adjust tone, and help adapt material for different audiences.

In this model, the opportunity comes from helping organizations **expand the reach of their content** by making it accessible to people in additional languages and regions. AI speeds up the translation process, while human oversight helps ensure that the meaning and tone remain accurate.

Why This Works Now

Global audiences are easier to reach than ever before. Businesses, online educators, and content creators often publish material that could be valuable to people in many different countries. However, producing content in multiple languages traditionally required professional translators and significant time.

AI tools have made translation much faster and more accessible.

For example, AI can help with:

- translating articles or blog posts into other languages
- adapting marketing content for different regions
- translating product descriptions for international markets
- generating subtitles for videos in multiple languages
- converting newsletters or guides into additional languages

These capabilities make it possible for creators and businesses to expand their reach without rebuilding their content from scratch.

Because many organizations want to reach global audiences but lack the time or expertise to do so, there is growing demand for people who can help manage the process.

Who This Is Best For

This starting point works well for people who:

- speak more than one language
- enjoy working with written communication
- are interested in global audiences or international markets
- pay attention to language details and tone

It can be especially valuable for bilingual individuals, translators, writers, or freelancers interested in language services.

However, even people who speak only one language can assist with parts of the workflow, such as organizing content, managing translation processes, or reviewing AI-generated drafts.
The key skill is ensuring that translated material **reads naturally and accurately in the target language**.

What You Need

The setup for offering AI-assisted translation services is relatively simple.
You need:

- an AI tool capable of translating or rewriting content
- access to the original material that needs translation
- the ability to review translations for clarity and accuracy
- familiarity with the audience or region the content is intended for

For video or audio content, you may also use tools that generate transcripts or subtitles.
Many translation projects begin with written content such as articles, websites, or marketing materials.

How to Start in 24 Hours

You can begin exploring this opportunity by practicing with a simple piece of content.
Step 1: Choose a piece of content
Examples might include:

- a short blog post
- a marketing email
- a social media post
- a product description

Step 2: Ask AI to translate the content

Generate a translation into another language.

Step 3: Review the translation

Check that the meaning and tone remain accurate.

Step 4: Adjust for clarity

Refine the language so it reads naturally for the target audience.

Step 5: Compare versions

Look at the original and translated versions to ensure the message remains consistent.

This exercise helps you understand how AI can support translation while still requiring human review.

How to Make Your First $100

Many small businesses want to reach customers in additional languages but do not know where to begin.

You might offer services such as:

- translating blog posts or articles
- translating product descriptions for online stores
- creating subtitles for videos
- adapting marketing messages for new audiences

For example:

A business might pay $50 to translate a set of product descriptions or short articles.

Completing two small translation projects could help you reach your first $100.

Because businesses increasingly operate online, multilingual content is becoming more valuable.

How to Grow It

If you enjoy working with languages, this opportunity can expand in several directions.

You might:

- specialize in translating content for specific industries
- focus on translating marketing or educational materials
- provide localization services for international audiences
- manage multilingual content for websites or online platforms
- build a small translation or localization agency

Over time, your ability to help organizations communicate across language barriers can become highly valuable.

Watch-Outs

One important challenge in translation is accuracy.
AI tools can translate text quickly, but they may miss cultural nuances or subtle meanings.
Human review is essential to ensure the message remains clear and appropriate.
Another challenge is tone.
Marketing or creative content may need additional adjustment to feel natural in different languages.
Finally, avoid assuming that direct translation is always enough.
Effective localization often requires adapting the message so it resonates with the audience.

Try This Next

Ask your AI tool:
"Translate this article into [another language] and adjust it so it sounds natural for readers in that language."
Then compare the original and translated versions to ensure the message remains clear.
This exercise will help you practice reviewing and refining AI-assisted translations.

Reflection Question
Think about the content you regularly see online.
How many valuable resources exist only in one language?
Helping creators and businesses share their ideas across languages can open entirely new audiences.

This is the **twenty-seventh of the 33 starting points**.
The next chapter explores another opportunity created by AI:
helping individuals and organizations organize and manage knowledge using AI-powered knowledge bases and documentation systems.

Starting Point #28

Building AI-Powered Knowledge Bases and Documentation Systems

Difficulty: Intermediate
Startup Cost: Low
Time to First Income: 2–4 weeks
Income Type: Service-based or Product-based

What It Is

Another opportunity created by AI is helping individuals and organizations **organize and manage information through AI-powered knowledge bases and documentation systems**.

Many businesses and teams accumulate large amounts of information over time. This may include internal documents, training materials, project notes, research, policies, and customer information.

Unfortunately, much of this information becomes difficult to locate or use effectively.

Employees may spend significant time searching for documents, repeating questions, or recreating information that already exists.

AI tools can help organize and structure this information in ways that make it easier to access and understand.

For example, AI can help summarize documents, categorize information, generate searchable knowledge bases, and assist with answering questions based on stored materials.

In this model, the opportunity comes from helping organizations **turn scattered information into structured knowledge systems**.

AI helps process and organize the material, while human guidance ensures the information is accurate, useful, and logically structured.

Why This Works Now

Modern organizations produce enormous amounts of information.

Emails, documents, meeting notes, project files, and internal resources accumulate quickly. Without proper organization, valuable knowledge becomes difficult to access.

AI tools now make it easier to analyze and organize large collections of information.

For example, AI can assist with:

- summarizing long documents
- organizing files into structured categories
- generating documentation from notes or transcripts
- creating searchable knowledge libraries
- answering questions based on stored information

These capabilities allow organizations to transform scattered information into systems that employees can actually use.

Because many businesses struggle with knowledge management, there is growing demand for people who can help design these systems.

Who This Is Best For

This starting point works well for people who:

- enjoy organizing complex information
- like building structured systems
- are interested in productivity and workplace efficiency
- pay attention to detail and documentation

It can be a good fit for consultants, project managers, technical writers, operations specialists, or freelancers interested in information systems.

You do not necessarily need advanced programming skills.

Many modern knowledge management platforms allow users to build structured systems using visual tools and AI-assisted organization.
The key skill is turning **disorganized information into clear, accessible knowledge**.

What You Need

The setup for building AI-assisted knowledge systems is relatively simple.
You need:

- an AI tool capable of summarizing and organizing information
- access to the documents or information that need organization
- a platform for storing and organizing the knowledge base
- the ability to structure information clearly

Many knowledge systems are built using documents, internal websites, or specialized platforms designed for knowledge management.
The goal is to make information easy to find, understand, and update.

How to Start in 24 Hours

You can begin exploring this opportunity by organizing a small collection of information.

Step 1: Choose a set of documents

Examples might include:

- training materials
- research notes
- project documentation
- meeting summaries

Step 2: Ask AI to summarize the documents

Identify the key points and major topics.

Step 3: Create categories
Organize the information into logical groups.
Step 4: Build a simple knowledge structure
Create sections that make it easy to locate specific information.
Step 5: Test the system
Ask questions and see whether the knowledge base helps users find the answers quickly.
This exercise helps you practice turning scattered information into a structured system.

How to Make Your First $100
Many organizations struggle with disorganized documentation.
You might offer services such as:

- organizing company documents into a knowledge base
- summarizing internal reports or materials
- creating documentation systems for teams
- building internal guides or training libraries

For example:
A small business might pay $50 to organize key documents into a structured internal guide.
Helping two clients improve their documentation systems could help you reach your first $100.
Because organized knowledge saves time and reduces confusion, businesses often see immediate value in these improvements.

How to Grow It
If you enjoy building knowledge systems, this opportunity can expand in several directions.
You might:

- specialize in knowledge systems for specific industries
- design documentation frameworks for organizations
- manage knowledge bases for growing companies
- develop templates for knowledge management systems
- combine documentation services with automation tools

Over time, knowledge management can become a highly valuable service within organizations that rely on complex information.

Watch-Outs

One common mistake is overcomplicating the system.
A knowledge base should make information easier to find, not harder.
Another challenge is keeping the information updated.
Documentation systems must be maintained over time so the information remains accurate and useful.
Finally, remember that technology alone does not solve the problem.
The success of a knowledge system depends on clear organization, thoughtful structure, and consistent maintenance.

Try This Next

Ask your AI tool:
"Organize these documents into a clear knowledge base structure with categories and summaries."
Review the structure and refine it so it makes sense for the intended users.

This exercise will help you practice building organized knowledge systems.

Reflection Question

Think about how much time people spend searching for information at work.

How much more efficient could a team become if that information were easy to find and understand?

Helping organizations organize their knowledge can create lasting value.

This is the **twenty-eighth of the 33 starting points**.

The next chapter explores another opportunity created by AI: **helping individuals and businesses analyze trends, insights, and opportunities using AI-assisted forecasting and research.**

Starting Point #29
AI-Assisted Research and Trend Analysis

Difficulty: Beginner to Intermediate
Startup Cost: Low
Time to First Income: 1–3 weeks
Income Type: Service-based or Product-based

What It Is

Another opportunity created by AI is helping individuals and businesses **research trends, analyze information, and identify opportunities**.

Many organizations rely on research to make decisions. They may need to understand market trends, customer preferences, industry changes, or emerging technologies. However, gathering and organizing large amounts of information can take significant time.

AI tools can help accelerate this process.

They can summarize articles, analyze reports, extract key insights, compare sources, and organize information into clear summaries.

In this model, the opportunity comes from helping people **turn large amounts of information into clear insights they can use to make decisions**.

AI helps process and summarize the data, while the human role involves verifying the information, interpreting the insights, and presenting them in a useful way.

Why This Works Now

The amount of information available online has grown dramatically.

Businesses, investors, entrepreneurs, and researchers often need to review articles, reports, market data, and news sources to stay informed.

This process can be time-consuming and overwhelming.
AI tools can assist by quickly scanning large volumes of information and identifying the most important ideas.
For example, AI can help with:

- summarizing long reports or research papers
- identifying emerging trends in an industry
- comparing products, competitors, or strategies
- analyzing customer feedback or reviews
- organizing research into structured summaries

These capabilities allow individuals and businesses to make decisions faster.
Because many people struggle to keep up with the constant flow of information, there is growing demand for services that help simplify research and highlight key insights.

Who This Is Best For

This starting point works well for people who:

- enjoy learning and researching new topics
- like analyzing information and identifying patterns
- are curious about business, technology, or social trends
- enjoy summarizing complex ideas clearly

It can be a good fit for freelancers, analysts, consultants, writers, students, or professionals interested in research.
You do not need to be a professional researcher to begin.
Many valuable research services focus on gathering information from reliable sources and organizing it into clear summaries that others can easily understand.
The key skill is turning **information into insight**.

What You Need

The setup for offering AI-assisted research services is relatively simple.

You need:

- an AI tool capable of summarizing and analyzing information
- access to articles, reports, or data sources related to the research topic
- the ability to evaluate sources and verify information
- a clear format for presenting your findings

Research reports are often delivered as summaries, presentations, or written briefs.

The value comes from clarity, organization, and useful insights.

How to Start in 24 Hours

You can begin exploring this opportunity by researching a simple topic.

Step 1: Choose an industry or topic

Examples might include:

- online education
- fitness trends
- small business marketing
- remote work tools

Step 2: Gather several articles or reports

Collect information from reputable sources.

Step 3: Ask AI to summarize the key ideas

Identify recurring patterns or trends.

Step 4: Organize the insights

Create a short report highlighting the most important findings.

Step 5: Present the results

Structure the report so it is easy to read and understand.

This exercise helps you practice turning scattered information into useful insights.

How to Make Your First $100

Many professionals and entrepreneurs need quick research summaries.

You might offer services such as:

- researching market trends for small businesses
- summarizing industry reports
- analyzing competitors for startups
- compiling research briefs on specific topics

For example:

A client might pay $50 for a short report summarizing trends in their industry.

Completing two research projects could help you reach your first $100.

Because decision-makers value clear information, well-organized research can be very useful.

How to Grow It

If you enjoy research and analysis, this opportunity can expand in several directions.

You might:

- specialize in research for specific industries
- produce regular trend reports or newsletters
- offer consulting based on research insights
- help businesses analyze customer feedback or reviews
- build research tools or databases for clients

Over time, research and trend analysis can become a valuable advisory service.

Organizations often rely on clear insights to guide their strategies and investments.

Watch-Outs

One challenge in research is accuracy.
AI tools can summarize information quickly, but they may occasionally misunderstand sources or overlook context.
Important insights should always be verified with reliable sources.
Another challenge is information overload.
The goal is not to collect as much information as possible, but to identify the most meaningful insights.
Finally, avoid presenting speculation as certainty.
Good research highlights patterns and possibilities while acknowledging uncertainty.

Try This Next

Ask your AI tool:
"Summarize the major trends currently shaping the [industry or topic] sector."
Review the results and compare them with several reliable sources.
This exercise will help you practice identifying patterns and insights.

Reflection Question

Think about the decisions people make in business, investing, or career planning.
How often do those decisions depend on understanding trends and reliable information?
Helping people interpret complex information can become a powerful and valuable service.

This is the **twenty-ninth of the 33 starting points**.
The next chapter explores another opportunity created by AI:

helping businesses analyze customer feedback, reviews, and data to improve products and services.

Starting Point #31
Automating Repetitive Tasks With AI

Difficulty: Beginner to Intermediate
Startup Cost: Low
Time to First Income: 1–3 weeks
Income Type: Service-based

What It Is

Another opportunity created by AI is helping individuals and businesses **automate repetitive tasks and workflows**. Many professionals spend a large portion of their day completing routine activities such as organizing emails, updating spreadsheets, responding to common messages, entering data, or transferring information between systems. While these tasks are necessary, they often take time away from more important work.

AI tools and automation platforms can help reduce this workload by performing certain tasks automatically.

For example, AI can assist with:

- organizing incoming emails
- generating responses to common questions
- summarizing meeting notes
- updating records or documents
- triggering actions when certain events occur

In this model, the opportunity comes from helping individuals and organizations **design simple automated workflows that save time and reduce manual effort**.

AI becomes part of a system that handles repetitive tasks automatically, while humans focus on higher-value work.

Why This Works Now

The number of digital tools people use at work has increased dramatically.

Professionals often manage multiple platforms such as email, messaging apps, customer relationship systems, project management tools, and spreadsheets.

These systems generate constant streams of tasks and notifications.

Many of these tasks follow predictable patterns.

For example:

- a new customer inquiry triggers a standard response
- a form submission creates a new record in a spreadsheet
- meeting notes need to be summarized and shared
- customer questions require similar answers

AI tools and automation platforms now make it possible to connect these systems and automate routine steps.

Because many organizations want to save time but do not know how to build these workflows, there is growing demand for people who can design and implement simple automation systems.

Who This Is Best For

This starting point works well for people who:

- enjoy improving systems and processes
- like solving efficiency problems
- are curious about digital tools and workflows
- enjoy experimenting with new technology

It can be a good fit for freelancers, operations specialists, virtual assistants, consultants, or anyone interested in productivity systems.

You do not need to be a professional programmer to begin.

Many automation tools allow users to build workflows through visual interfaces rather than complex code.

The key skill is recognizing **which tasks can be automated and designing systems that handle them effectively**.

What You Need

The setup for building AI-assisted automation systems is relatively simple.

You need:

- an AI tool that can assist with text generation or data processing
- an automation platform capable of connecting different tools
- access to the workflows that need improvement
- the ability to design and test simple systems

Automation often involves connecting existing tools so information flows automatically between them.

The goal is to reduce repetitive work while maintaining accuracy.

How to Start in 24 Hours

You can begin exploring this opportunity by automating a small task.

Step 1: Identify a repetitive activity

Examples might include:

- sending similar email responses
- summarizing meeting notes
- organizing incoming requests
- updating information in multiple systems

Step 2: Map the workflow

Write down the steps that currently happen manually.

Step 3: Ask AI how the process could be automated

Identify which parts could be handled automatically.

Step 4: Build a simple workflow

Use an automation tool to connect the steps.

Step 5: Test the system
Confirm that the automation works reliably.
This exercise helps you see how small improvements can save time and reduce manual effort.

How to Make Your First $100
Many small businesses and professionals want to automate tasks but do not know where to begin.
You might offer services such as:

- automating email responses
- organizing incoming leads or inquiries
- creating workflows for handling customer requests
- connecting tools that currently require manual updates

For example:
A business might pay $50 to set up a simple automation that organizes incoming inquiries and sends an automatic reply.
Helping two clients implement small automation systems could help you reach your first $100.
Because automation can save time every day, businesses often see immediate value in these improvements.

How to Grow It
If you enjoy designing automation systems, this opportunity can expand significantly.
You might:

- specialize in workflow automation for specific industries
- build more advanced automation systems for organizations
- create automation templates that others can use

- offer ongoing support for maintaining automation systems
- develop consulting services around operational efficiency

Over time, automation expertise can become highly valuable as organizations look for ways to improve productivity.

Watch-Outs

One challenge in automation is designing systems that are too complicated.

The best automation systems are usually simple, reliable, and easy to maintain.

Another challenge is ensuring that automated processes still produce accurate results.

Automated workflows should be tested carefully before they are relied upon.

Finally, remember that not every task should be automated. Human judgment is still essential for work that requires creativity, empathy, or complex decision-making.

Try This Next

Ask your AI tool:

"Identify five repetitive tasks that could potentially be automated in a small business workflow."

Review the suggestions and choose one that could realistically be simplified.

This exercise will help you begin thinking like an automation designer.

Reflection Question

Think about how many repetitive tasks occur in a typical workday.

What would happen if even a few of those tasks were handled automatically?

Helping people save time through automation can create meaningful value.

This is the **thirty-first of the 33 starting points**.
The next chapter explores another opportunity created by AI: **creating and managing AI-powered assistants that help businesses interact with customers and audiences.**

Starting Point #31
Automating Repetitive Tasks With AI

Difficulty: Beginner to Intermediate
Startup Cost: Low
Time to First Income: 1–3 weeks
Income Type: Service-based

What It Is

Another opportunity created by AI is helping individuals and businesses **automate repetitive tasks and workflows**. Many professionals spend a large portion of their day completing routine activities such as organizing emails, updating spreadsheets, responding to common messages, entering data, or transferring information between systems. While these tasks are necessary, they often take time away from more important work.

AI tools and automation platforms can help reduce this workload by performing certain tasks automatically.

For example, AI can assist with:

- organizing incoming emails
- generating responses to common questions
- summarizing meeting notes
- updating records or documents
- triggering actions when certain events occur

In this model, the opportunity comes from helping individuals and organizations **design simple automated workflows that save time and reduce manual effort**.

AI becomes part of a system that handles repetitive tasks automatically, while humans focus on higher-value work.

Why This Works Now

The number of digital tools people use at work has increased dramatically.

Professionals often manage multiple platforms such as email, messaging apps, customer relationship systems, project management tools, and spreadsheets.
These systems generate constant streams of tasks and notifications.
Many of these tasks follow predictable patterns.
For example:

- a new customer inquiry triggers a standard response
- a form submission creates a new record in a spreadsheet
- meeting notes need to be summarized and shared
- customer questions require similar answers

AI tools and automation platforms now make it possible to connect these systems and automate routine steps.
Because many organizations want to save time but do not know how to build these workflows, there is growing demand for people who can design and implement simple automation systems.

Who This Is Best For

This starting point works well for people who:

- enjoy improving systems and processes
- like solving efficiency problems
- are curious about digital tools and workflows
- enjoy experimenting with new technology

It can be a good fit for freelancers, operations specialists, virtual assistants, consultants, or anyone interested in productivity systems.
You do not need to be a professional programmer to begin.
Many automation tools allow users to build workflows through visual interfaces rather than complex code.

The key skill is recognizing **which tasks can be automated and designing systems that handle them effectively**.

What You Need

The setup for building AI-assisted automation systems is relatively simple.

You need:

- an AI tool that can assist with text generation or data processing
- an automation platform capable of connecting different tools
- access to the workflows that need improvement
- the ability to design and test simple systems

Automation often involves connecting existing tools so information flows automatically between them.

The goal is to reduce repetitive work while maintaining accuracy.

How to Start in 24 Hours

You can begin exploring this opportunity by automating a small task.

Step 1: Identify a repetitive activity

Examples might include:

- sending similar email responses
- summarizing meeting notes
- organizing incoming requests
- updating information in multiple systems

Step 2: Map the workflow

Write down the steps that currently happen manually.

Step 3: Ask AI how the process could be automated

Identify which parts could be handled automatically.

Step 4: Build a simple workflow

Use an automation tool to connect the steps.

Step 5: Test the system
Confirm that the automation works reliably.
This exercise helps you see how small improvements can save time and reduce manual effort.

How to Make Your First $100

Many small businesses and professionals want to automate tasks but do not know where to begin.
You might offer services such as:

- automating email responses
- organizing incoming leads or inquiries
- creating workflows for handling customer requests
- connecting tools that currently require manual updates

For example:
A business might pay $50 to set up a simple automation that organizes incoming inquiries and sends an automatic reply.
Helping two clients implement small automation systems could help you reach your first $100.
Because automation can save time every day, businesses often see immediate value in these improvements.

How to Grow It

If you enjoy designing automation systems, this opportunity can expand significantly.
You might:

- specialize in workflow automation for specific industries
- build more advanced automation systems for organizations
- create automation templates that others can use

- offer ongoing support for maintaining automation systems
- develop consulting services around operational efficiency

Over time, automation expertise can become highly valuable as organizations look for ways to improve productivity.

Watch-Outs

One challenge in automation is designing systems that are too complicated.

The best automation systems are usually simple, reliable, and easy to maintain.

Another challenge is ensuring that automated processes still produce accurate results.

Automated workflows should be tested carefully before they are relied upon.

Finally, remember that not every task should be automated.

Human judgment is still essential for work that requires creativity, empathy, or complex decision-making.

Try This Next

Ask your AI tool:

"Identify five repetitive tasks that could potentially be automated in a small business workflow."

Review the suggestions and choose one that could realistically be simplified.

This exercise will help you begin thinking like an automation designer.

Reflection Question

Think about how many repetitive tasks occur in a typical workday.

What would happen if even a few of those tasks were handled automatically?

Helping people save time through automation can create meaningful value.

This is the **thirty-first of the 33 starting points**.
The next chapter explores another opportunity created by AI: **creating and managing AI-powered assistants that help businesses interact with customers and audiences.**

Starting Point #32
Creating and Managing AI-Powered Assistants

Difficulty: Beginner to Intermediate
Startup Cost: Low
Time to First Income: 1–3 weeks
Income Type: Service-based or Product-based

What It Is

Another opportunity created by AI is helping businesses and organizations **create and manage AI-powered assistants** that interact with customers, clients, or audiences.

Many businesses receive frequent questions about products, services, pricing, policies, or support issues.

Responding to these questions one at a time can take a significant amount of time.

AI assistants can help answer common questions, guide users through information, and provide useful responses automatically.

These assistants may appear as chatbots on websites, automated messaging systems, or AI-powered support tools built into customer service platforms.

For example, AI assistants can help:

- answer frequently asked questions
- guide customers through product information
- help users navigate websites or services
- provide automated support responses
- collect information before connecting a customer with a human representative

In this model, the opportunity comes from helping businesses **design, implement, and maintain AI assistants that improve communication and reduce workload**.

AI provides the conversational capability, while human guidance helps ensure that the assistant is accurate, helpful, and appropriate for the business.

Why This Works Now

Customer communication now happens across many platforms.

Businesses interact with customers through websites, email, social media, messaging apps, and online support systems.

This creates a large volume of questions and support requests.

AI-powered assistants can help businesses respond more quickly and consistently.

For example, AI assistants can:

- answer common customer questions instantly
- provide support outside of normal business hours
- handle large numbers of simple inquiries
- route complex issues to human staff
- collect useful information before support conversations begin

Because businesses want faster response times while managing support costs, AI assistants have become increasingly attractive.

However, many companies still need help designing assistants that communicate clearly and provide genuinely useful answers.

Who This Is Best For

This starting point works well for people who:

- enjoy designing systems that help others find information
- are interested in communication and customer experience

- like organizing knowledge into clear responses
- enjoy experimenting with technology and digital tools

It can be a good fit for freelancers, customer support specialists, marketers, consultants, or technology enthusiasts.

You do not need to be an advanced programmer to begin. Many AI assistant platforms allow users to build conversational systems using simple tools and structured prompts.

The key skill is designing conversations that are **clear, helpful, and easy for users to follow**.

What You Need

The setup for creating AI-powered assistants is relatively simple.

You need:

- an AI platform capable of creating conversational assistants
- access to the information the assistant will use to answer questions
- the ability to organize responses clearly
- a platform where the assistant will interact with users

Most AI assistants rely on structured information such as frequently asked questions, product details, or support documentation.

The quality of the assistant depends heavily on how well this information is organized.

How to Start in 24 Hours

You can begin exploring this opportunity by designing a simple assistant for a common scenario.

Step 1: Choose a topic
Examples might include:

- answering frequently asked questions for a business
- helping users understand a product or service
- guiding visitors through a website

Step 2: Gather common questions
List the questions customers or users ask most often.
Step 3: Write clear responses
Use AI to help draft concise and helpful answers.
Step 4: Build a basic assistant
Use an AI platform to create a simple conversational flow.
Step 5: Test the assistant
Interact with it as a user would and refine the responses.
This exercise helps you learn how AI assistants are designed and improved.

How to Make Your First $100
Many small businesses want to offer faster customer responses but lack the time or technical knowledge to build AI assistants.
You might offer services such as:

- creating FAQ chatbots for websites
- building messaging assistants for businesses
- organizing knowledge for AI support systems
- improving existing chatbot responses

For example:
A business might pay $50 to set up a basic assistant that answers common customer questions.
Helping two clients build simple AI assistants could help you reach your first $100.
Because automated assistants can reduce support workload, businesses often see clear value in these systems.

How to Grow It

If you enjoy building AI assistants, this opportunity can expand significantly.

You might:

- specialize in assistants for customer support
- design assistants for specific industries
- manage and improve assistants over time
- build assistants that integrate with business tools
- develop more advanced conversational systems

Over time, AI assistants may become a common part of how businesses interact with customers.

Those who understand how to design effective assistants may find growing opportunities in this area.

Watch-Outs

One challenge in designing AI assistants is ensuring that the responses are accurate.

If an assistant provides incorrect information, it can quickly damage trust.

Another challenge is designing conversations that feel natural and useful.

Users should be able to get answers easily rather than feeling trapped in confusing loops or vague replies.

Finally, AI assistants should complement human support rather than fully replace it.

Some situations still require human judgment, empathy, and problem-solving.

Try This Next

Ask your AI tool:

"Generate ten common customer questions a business might receive about its products or services."

Then write clear responses to those questions.
This exercise will help you begin thinking about how AI assistants handle conversations.

Reflection Question

Think about the last time you interacted with a chatbot or automated assistant.
Was the experience helpful or frustrating?
Designing assistants that truly help users can become an important skill as AI becomes more integrated into everyday business communication.

This is the **thirty-second of the 33 starting points**.
The final chapter explores an important opportunity created by AI:
teaching others how to use AI effectively and responsibly to improve their work, businesses, and daily lives.

Starting Point #33
Teaching Others How to Use AI

Difficulty: Beginner to Intermediate
Startup Cost: Low
Time to First Income: 1–3 weeks
Income Type: Service-based or Product-based

What It Is

One of the most powerful opportunities created by AI is helping others **learn how to use AI effectively**.

While AI tools have become widely available, many people still feel unsure about how to use them in practical ways. They may know the technology exists, but they do not yet understand how it can help them in their work, businesses, or daily lives.

This creates a growing need for people who can teach practical AI skills.

Teaching AI does not necessarily mean explaining complex technical concepts. More often, it means showing others how to use AI tools to solve real problems.

For example, people may want to learn how to use AI to:

- write and edit documents
- generate ideas or outlines
- organize information
- automate routine tasks
- improve productivity
- create content or marketing materials

In this model, the opportunity comes from helping people **understand how AI can be applied to their specific needs**.

AI becomes the tool being taught, while the instructor helps learners discover practical ways to use it well.

Why This Works Now
AI adoption is growing rapidly across many industries. However, the technology is advancing faster than most people can keep up with. Many professionals, students, and entrepreneurs feel that they should understand AI but are not sure where to begin.
Organizations are also beginning to recognize that their teams need AI skills.
This creates demand for people who can explain AI tools in ways that are practical and easy to understand.
For example, educators or trainers may help others:

- learn the basics of using AI tools
- develop effective prompts and workflows
- integrate AI into daily work tasks
- explore ethical and responsible use of AI
- understand how AI can support their profession

Because AI is still relatively new for many people, even simple guidance can provide meaningful value.

Who This Is Best For
This starting point works well for people who:

- enjoy teaching or explaining ideas
- like helping others learn new skills
- are curious about technology and innovation
- communicate clearly and patiently

It can be a good fit for educators, trainers, consultants, content creators, or professionals who enjoy sharing knowledge.
You do not need to be an expert in artificial intelligence to begin.
In many cases, effective teachers are simply people who have spent time learning the tools and can explain them clearly to others.

The key skill is translating technology into **practical, understandable steps**.

What You Need

The setup for teaching AI skills is relatively simple.
You need:

- familiarity with one or more AI tools
- the ability to demonstrate how those tools work
- clear explanations and examples
- a platform or format for teaching others

Teaching may take many forms, including workshops, online courses, coaching sessions, guides, or educational content. The value comes from helping people move from confusion to confidence when using AI tools.

How to Start in 24 Hours

You can begin exploring this opportunity by teaching a simple AI skill.

Step 1: Choose a small topic

Examples might include:

- how to write better prompts
- how to summarize information using AI
- how to generate ideas with AI tools

Step 2: Create a short lesson

Explain the concept in a simple, step-by-step format.

Step 3: Demonstrate the tool

Show how the AI tool produces useful results.

Step 4: Let someone try it

Ask a friend, colleague, or small group to test the lesson.

Step 5: Refine the explanation

Improve the lesson based on their questions or feedback.
This exercise helps you practice turning your knowledge into teachable guidance.

How to Make Your First $100

Many people are willing to pay for help learning new tools that can improve their work.

You might offer services such as:

- teaching small AI workshops
- offering one-on-one coaching sessions
- creating beginner AI tutorials
- helping professionals apply AI to their jobs

For example:

You might charge $50 for a short AI training session or consultation.

Helping two people learn how to use AI tools effectively could help you reach your first $100.

Because the demand for AI education is growing quickly, opportunities in this area may continue to expand.

How to Grow It

If you enjoy teaching others, this opportunity can expand in many directions.

You might:

- create courses on AI skills
- host workshops for businesses or organizations
- build online communities around learning AI
- develop educational content or guides
- specialize in AI training for specific industries

Over time, teaching AI can evolve into consulting, education programs, or larger training businesses.

As AI becomes more integrated into everyday work, people who help others understand and use these tools may play an important role in shaping how the technology is adopted.

Watch-Outs

One challenge in teaching AI is staying current.

AI tools evolve quickly, so instructors need to keep learning and updating their knowledge.
Another challenge is overwhelming beginners with too much technical information.
Effective teaching focuses on simple, practical examples that people can apply immediately.
Finally, remember that AI should be used responsibly.
Helping people understand the ethical and thoughtful use of AI is just as important as teaching the tools themselves.

Try This Next
Ask your AI tool:
“Create a simple lesson that teaches someone how to use AI to save time on everyday tasks.”
Review the lesson and imagine how you would explain it to someone who has never used AI before.
This exercise will help you begin thinking like an AI teacher.

Reflection Question
Think about how many people around you are still unsure how to use AI tools effectively.
What difference could it make if they had someone who could guide them through the learning process?
Helping others learn how to use AI may become one of the most meaningful opportunities created by this technology.

This is the **thirty-third of the 33 starting points**.
Together, these ideas represent a wide range of ways people are beginning to create value with AI.
The real opportunity is not simply using AI itself.
It is learning how to apply it thoughtfully to real problems, real people, and real opportunities.

Conclusion

Where AI and Opportunity Meet

Throughout this book, you explored **33 different starting points for making money with AI**.

Some of these ideas may have immediately caught your attention. Others may have felt less relevant to your interests or skills. That is completely normal.

The goal of this book was never to suggest that you should pursue all thirty-three opportunities. Instead, the purpose was to show that **AI is creating a wide range of possibilities across many different types of work**.

Some opportunities involve writing and content creation. Others focus on automation, research, education, or digital products.

Some involve services, while others can evolve into scalable products or businesses.

The important idea is this:

AI is not just a tool for technology companies. It is becoming a tool for everyone.

People who learn how to use it thoughtfully can apply it to many different kinds of work.

You Do Not Need to Master Everything

One common mistake people make when learning about AI is believing they must understand everything before they begin.

In reality, progress usually happens in a different way.

Most people start by exploring **one small idea**.

They experiment.

They test.

They learn what works and what does not.

Over time, their understanding grows.

The same approach works when exploring the opportunities in this book.
You do not need to master thirty-three ideas.
You only need to begin with **one starting point**.

AI Rewards Curiosity

The people who benefit most from new technologies are rarely those who wait until everything is perfect or fully understood.
Instead, they tend to remain curious.
They try new tools.
They explore possibilities.
They pay attention to how technology can solve real problems.
AI is no different.
The tools will continue to change.
New platforms will appear.
Capabilities will expand.
But the underlying opportunity will remain the same:
People who learn how to apply AI creatively will be able to create value in new ways.

The Human Role Still Matters

It is easy to think of AI as replacing human work.
But in most cases, the real opportunity comes from **combining human judgment with AI capabilities**.
AI can generate ideas, analyze information, summarize content, and automate certain tasks.
But humans still provide:

- creativity
- context
- judgment
- empathy
- strategy

In many of the starting points in this book, the most valuable work happens when **AI assists a person rather than replacing them**.
This partnership between human thinking and machine assistance may become one of the defining features of the modern economy.

Start Small
If you feel unsure where to begin, choose the simplest step.
Pick one idea from this book and ask yourself:
- Could I experiment with this for one hour?
- Could I test this idea with one small project?
- Could I help one person solve a problem using AI?

Small experiments often lead to larger opportunities.
The first goal is not perfection.
The goal is **experience**.

The Future Is Still Being Written
Artificial intelligence is changing how people work, create, and build opportunities.
Many of the opportunities that will exist in the future have not yet been discovered.
The people who discover them will likely be those who continue experimenting, learning, and adapting.
In that sense, this book is not meant to be a final answer.
It is meant to be **a set of starting points**.
Your path may combine several of these ideas.
You may adapt them into something new.
You may discover opportunities that did not exist when this book was written.
That is part of the process.

One Final Thought
Technology alone rarely creates opportunity.

Opportunity comes from how people choose to use technology to help others, solve problems, and create value.
AI is simply a powerful new tool.
The real question is not what AI can do.
The real question is:
What will you choose to do with it?
The future of AI is still being created.
And now, you have **33 places to begin.**

APENDIX

Your First AI Money Experiment

Ideas become valuable when they are tested.
Throughout this book, you explored thirty-three different starting points for making money with AI. You do not need to try all of them. The most effective way to begin is to choose **one idea and experiment with it**.
The goal is not to build a perfect business immediately.
The goal is to learn how AI can help you create value.
If you are unsure where to begin, try the following simple experiment.

The 7-Day AI Money Experiment

This short exercise is designed to help you move from ideas to action.
By the end of the week, you will have taken the first real steps toward applying AI to a practical opportunity.

Day 1 — Choose Your Starting Point

Review the thirty-three starting points in this book and select the one that interests you the most.
Do not worry about choosing the perfect idea. Curiosity is often the best place to begin.

Day 2 — Brainstorm with AI

Use an AI tool to generate ideas related to your chosen starting point.
For example, you might ask:
“Generate ten ways someone could use this idea to help people solve a problem.”
Review the responses and identify the ideas that feel most practical.

Day 3 — Identify a Real Problem

Select one idea and think about the specific problem it could solve.
Ask yourself:

- Who might need this?
- What problem does it help solve?
- Why might someone find it useful?

Clear problems often lead to valuable solutions.

Day 4 — Build a Simple Version
Create the simplest version of your idea.
This might involve:

- drafting a small digital resource
- outlining a service you could offer
- creating a template, checklist, or guide
- building a basic prototype

Do not focus on perfection. Focus on **creating something real**.

Day 5 — Share the Idea
Show your idea to someone who might benefit from it.
Ask questions such as:

- Would this be useful to you?
- What would make it better?
- Is there something missing?

Feedback often reveals insights you may not have considered.

Day 6 — Improve the Concept
Use what you learned to refine the idea.
Many successful projects begin as simple experiments and improve over time.
Small adjustments can make a big difference.

Day 7 — Take One Real Step

Take one concrete step toward offering the idea to others.
This might mean:

- sharing it online
- offering the service to a potential client
- listing the digital product on a platform
- continuing to develop the concept

The purpose is not to build a full business in one week.
The purpose is to **start learning by doing**.

The Real Opportunity

Artificial intelligence is a powerful tool, but tools only become valuable when they are used to solve real problems for real people.

Many successful projects begin with a simple experiment.
This could be the beginning of yours.

A Quick Request

If you found value in this book, I would greatly appreciate it if you considered leaving a brief review.

Reviews help other readers discover books that may help them explore new ideas and opportunities.

Even a short review sharing what you found useful can make a meaningful difference.

Thank you for taking the time to read this book and explore the possibilities that artificial intelligence is creating.

A Letter from BORI TRIII

If you have reached this point in the book, thank you for spending your time exploring these ideas.

Artificial intelligence is often discussed as if it were something distant or complicated—something reserved for engineers, scientists, or technology companies.

But the truth is much simpler.

AI is becoming a tool that ordinary people can use in extraordinary ways.

Throughout this book, you explored thirty-three different starting points. Each one represents a small window into how AI might be used to create value, solve problems, or open new opportunities.

Some of those ideas may remain just ideas.

Others may spark curiosity.

And perhaps one or two may lead you to try something new.

That is enough.

Every meaningful project, business, or innovation usually begins the same way: with someone experimenting with an idea that seems worth exploring.

Artificial intelligence will continue to evolve.

New tools will appear.

New possibilities will emerge.

Some things that feel impressive today will become ordinary tomorrow.

But one thing is unlikely to change.

Technology alone does not create opportunity.

People do.

People who are curious.

People who are willing to learn.

People who are willing to experiment with new tools and ask new questions.

If this book helped you think differently about what might be possible with AI, then it has served its purpose.
The future of this technology will not be shaped only by large companies or complex algorithms.
It will also be shaped by individuals who discover practical, creative ways to apply these tools in everyday life.
Perhaps you will become one of those people.
Where these ideas lead is entirely up to you.
But now you know where to begin.
— **BORI TRIII**

Explore the Series

www.aiandibooks.com

Your home for the collection, bonus reflections, community editions, and future releases.

Learn More About BORI TRIII Media House

www.boritriii.com

Discover upcoming projects, multimedia releases, author events, and the creative ecosystem behind the AI and I™ series.

Follow on Instagram

@aiandibooks — follow for daily reflections born from the edge of thought and technology, behind-the-scenes looks at the **AI and I™** series, new visuals from the In-Between, and ongoing book updates, follow along on Instagram:

@boritriii — the creative studio behind the work: design, storytelling, and the evolving world of **BORI TRIII Media House**.

www.ingramcontent.com/pod-product-compliance
Lightning Source LLC
LaVergne TN
LVHW020712110826
845149LV00012B/2226
9781971711041